W9-BXE-651

LONDON PUBLIC LIBRARY
20 EAST FIRST STREET
3/99 LONDON, OHIO 43140

WORLD HISTORY SERIES ■ ■ ■

The Renaissance

Titles in the World History Series

The Age of Augustus
The Age of Feudalism
The Age of Pericles
The Alamo
America in the 1960s
The American Frontier
The American Revolution
Ancient Greece
The Ancient Near East
Architecture
Aztec Civilization
The Battle of the
    Little Bighorn
The Black Death
The Byzantine Empire
Caesar's Conquest of Gaul
The California Gold Rush
The Chinese Cultural
    Revolution
The Civil Rights Movement
The Collapse of the
    Roman Republic
The Conquest of Mexico
The Crimean War
The Crusades
The Cuban Missile Crisis
The Cuban Revolution
The Early Middle Ages
Egypt of the Pharaohs
Elizabethan England
The End of the Cold War
The French and Indian War
The French Revolution
The Glorious Revolution
The Great Depression
Greek and Roman
    Mythology
Greek and Roman Science

Greek and Roman Theater
The History of Slavery
Hitler's Reich
The Hundred Years' War
The Industrial Revolution
The Inquisition
The Italian Renaissance
The Late Middle Ages
The Lewis and Clark
    Expedition
The Mexican Revolution
The Mexican War of
    Independence
Modern Japan
The Mongol Empire
The Persian Empire
The Punic Wars
The Reformation
The Relocation of the
    North American Indian
The Renaissance
The Roaring Twenties
The Roman Empire
The Roman Republic
Roosevelt and the New Deal
The Russian Revolution
Russia of the Tsars
The Scientific Revolution
The Spread of Islam
The Stone Age
Traditional Africa
Traditional Japan
The Travels of Marco Polo
Twentieth Century Science
The Wars of the Roses
The Watts Riot
Women's Suffrage

The Renaissance

by
James A. Corrick

WITHDRAWN

Lucent Books, P.O. Box 289011, San Diego, CA 92198-9011

For Dorothy Dunnett, whose novels about
Francis Crawford of Lymond and Nicholas
vander Poele bring the Renaissance to life.

Library of Congress Cataloging-in-Publication Data

Corrick, James A.
    The Renaissance / by James A. Corrick
       p. cm.—(World history series)
    Includes bibliographical references and index.
    Summary: Traces developments in European art, architecture, music, literature, philosophy, science, and exploration between 1300 and 1600.
    ISBN 1-56006-311-4 (alk. paper)
    1. Renaissance—Juvenile literature. [1. Renaissance.]
I.Title. II. Series.
CB361.C67   1998
940.2'1—DC21   97-27261
                                     CIP
                                     AC

Copyright 1998 by Lucent Books, Inc., P.O. Box 289011,
San Diego, California 92198-9011

Printed in the U.S.A.

No part of this book may be reproduced or used in any other form or by any other means, electrical, mechanical, or otherwise, including, but not limited to, photocopy, recording, or any information storage and retrieval system, without prior written permission from the publisher.

Contents

Foreword

Each year on the first day of school, nearly every history teacher faces the task of explaining why his or her students should study history. One logical answer to this question is that exploring what happened in our past explains how the things we often take for granted—our customs, ideas, and institutions—came to be. As statesman and historian Winston Churchill put it, "Every nation or group of nations has its own tale to tell. Knowledge of the trials and struggles is necessary to all who would comprehend the problems, perils, challenges, and opportunities which confront us today." Thus, a study of history puts modern ideas and institutions in perspective. For example, though the founders of the United States were talented and creative thinkers, they clearly did not invent the concept of democracy. Instead, they adapted some democratic ideas that had originated in ancient Greece and with which the Romans, the British, and others had experimented. An exploration of these cultures, then, reveals their very real connection to us through institutions that continue to shape our daily lives.

Another reason often given for studying history is the idea that lessons exist in the past from which contemporary societies can benefit and learn. This idea, although controversial, has always been an intriguing one for historians. Those who agree that society can benefit from the past often quote philosopher George Santayana's famous statement, "Those who cannot remember the past are condemned to repeat it." Historians who ascribe to Santayana's philosophy believe that, for example, studying the events that led up to the major world wars or other significant historical events would allow society to chart a different and more favorable course in the future.

Just as difficult as convincing students to realize the importance of studying history is the search for useful and interesting supplementary materials that present historical events in a context that can be easily understood. The volumes in Lucent Books' World History Series attempt to present a broad, balanced, and penetrating view of the march of history. Ancient Egypt's important wars and rulers, for example, are presented against the rich and colorful backdrop of Egyptian religious, social, and cultural developments. The series engages the reader by enhancing historical events with these cultural contexts. For example, in *Ancient Greece*, the text covers the role of women in that society. Slavery is discussed in *The Roman Empire*, as well as how slaves earned their freedom. The numerous and varied aspects of everyday life in these and other societies are explored in each volume of the series. Additionally, the series covers the major political, cultural, and philosophical ideas as the torch of civilization is passed from ancient Mesopotamia and Egypt, through Greece, Rome, Medieval Europe, and other world cultures, to the modern day.

The material in the series is formatted in a thorough, precise, and organized manner. Each volume offers the reader a comprehensive and clearly written overview of an important historical event or period. The topic under discussion is placed in a broad historical context. For example, *The Italian Renaissance* begins with a discussion of the High Middle Ages and the loss of central control that allowed certain Italian cities to develop artistically. The book ends by looking forward to the Reformation and interpreting the societal changes that grew out of the Renaissance. Thus, students are not only involved in an historical era, but also enveloped by the events leading up to that era and the events following it.

One important and unique feature in the World History Series is the primary and secondary source quotations that richly supplement each volume. These quotes are useful in a number of ways. First, they allow students access to sources they would not normally be exposed to because of the difficulty and obscurity of the original source. The quotations range from interesting anecdotes to farsighted cultural perspectives and are drawn from historical witnesses both past and present. Second, the quotes demonstrate how and where historians themselves derive their information on the past as they strive to reach a consensus on historical events. Lastly, all of the quotes are footnoted, familiarizing students with the citation process and allowing them to verify quotes and/or look up the original source if the quote piques their interest.

Finally, the books in the World History Series provide a detailed launching point for further research. Each book contains a bibliography specifically geared toward student research. A second, annotated bibliography introduces students to all the sources the author consulted when compiling the book. A chronology of important dates gives students an overview, at a glance, of the topic covered. Where applicable, a glossary of terms is included.

In short, the series is designed not only to acquaint readers with the basics of history, but also to make them aware that their lives are a part of an ongoing human saga. Perhaps they will then come to the same realization as famed historian Arnold Toynbee. In his monumental work, *A Study of History*, he wrote about becoming aware of history flowing through him in a mighty current, and of his own life "welling like a wave in the flow of this vast tide."

Important Dates in the History of the Renaissance

1265	1285	1305	1325	1345	1365	1385	1405	1425	1445

ca. 1307
Dante begins writing the *Divine Comedy*.

1341
The Roman Senate crowns Petrarch poet laureate.

1348
Boccaccio begins writing the *Decameron*.

ca. 1349
Petrarch assembles his sonnets in the *Canzoniere*.

1380
Venice defeats Genoa.

ca. 1387
Chaucer starts *The Canterbury Tales*.

1421
Prince Henry the Navigator begins sending Portuguese ships south to find a way around Africa to India.

1434
Cosimo de' Medici becomes ruler of Florence.

1439
The Platonic Academy is founded; the first standing army is formed in France.

1441
The African slave trade begins.

ca. 1450
The printing press is invented.

1453
Constantinople falls to the Ottoman Turks, and Greek-speaking refugees flee to Italy.

1461
Louis XI becomes king of France.

1469
Lorenzo de' Medici becomes ruler of Florence.

1479
Ferdinand and Isabella unite the kingdoms of Aragon and Castile to form Spain.

1483
Ficino's translation of Plato is published.

1485
Henry VII, the first Tudor king, takes the English throne.

1486
Pico writes the *Oration on the Dignity of Man*.

1492
Christopher Columbus, sailing for Spain, reaches the Americas.

1495–1497
Leonardo paints the *Last Supper*.

ca. 1497
John Cabot sails from England and discovers Newfoundland and Nova Scotia.

1498
Vasco da Gama of Portugal reaches India by sailing around Africa.

1499
Michelangelo finishes the *Pietà*.

1504
Michelangelo finishes *David*.

1507
The first map showing the New World as a separate continent and calling the land America appears.

1508
Michelangelo begins work on the ceiling of the Sistine Chapel.

1509
Erasmus publishes *The Praise of Folly*.

1513
Machiavelli writes *The Prince*.

1517
Martin Luther draws up his ninety-five theses.

| 1465 | 1485 | 1505 | 1525 | 1545 | 1565 | 1585 | 1605 | 1625 | 1633 |

1521
Martin Luther is excommunicated by the Catholic Church; Hernando Cortés conquers the Aztecs.

1522
The Magellan expedition completes the first circumnavigation of the earth.

1530
The College of France is founded.

1533
Francisco Pizarro conquers the Incas.

1534
Cartier discovers the Gulf of St. Lawrence and claims Canada for France.

1543
Copernicus's *On the Revolutions of the Heavenly Spheres* and Vesalius's *On the Structure of the Human Body* are published.

1545
Girolamo Cardano publishes the first modern algebra text, *The Great Art.*

1569
The first maps using the Mercator projection are published.

1582
The Gregorian calendar is introduced.

1586
Simon Stevin introduces decimals.

1587
Marlowe's first play, *Tamburlaine the Great,* appears.

1588
The English defeat the Spanish Armada.

ca. 1589
Shakespeare begins writing plays with the three parts of *Henry VI.*

1590
The compound microscope is invented.

1591
Galileo writes *On Motion,* and François Viète proposes a language for algebra.

ca. 1600
Shakespeare writes *Hamlet;* the English East India Company is founded.

1602
The Dutch East India Company is founded.

1605
The first part of Cervantes's *Don Quixote* appears, and Sir Francis Bacon writes *Advancement of Learning.*

1607
The English settle Jamestown in Virginia.

1608
The telescope is invented.

1609–1610
Kepler publishes *New Astronomy;* Galileo builds a telescope, views the moon's surface, discovers the four large moons of Jupiter, and studies the phases of Venus.

1615
The second part of Cervantes's *Don Quixote* appears.

1620
Sir Francis Bacon writes *Novum Organum.*

1632–1633
Galileo publishes *Dialogue on the Two Great World Systems;* tried by the church for heresy, he publicly renounces Copernicanism.

The New Age

It was the beginning of the fourteenth century, and the Middle Ages, or medieval period, which had lasted almost a thousand years since the fall of Rome, were about to give way to the Renaissance, one of the great cultural movements of history. Beginning in Italy in the 1300s, it spread rapidly throughout much of Europe during the next three hundred years. Seldom has so much happened in such a brief period; these were centuries filled with dramatic change and achievement. Out of this activity grew the modern world, for the Renaissance laid the economic, political, artistic, and scientific foundations of current Western civilization.

The Roots of the Renaissance

To those living during the Renaissance, their age was linked not with the Middle Ages, which they mistakenly viewed as a period of ignorance, but with that of ancient Greece and Rome. They believed that only the ancients had reached the same level of achievement. Indeed, the Renaissance saw itself as a revival or rebirth of the old Greek and Roman culture, and from this idea of a classical revival came the very name "Renaissance," French for "rebirth."

In reality, many of the roots of the Renaissance were in the Middle Ages. Interest in ancient Greece and Rome came from medieval students and scholars who had discovered Arabic translations of classical works in Muslim-controlled Spain and brought them north. Even some important inventions were medieval in origin. The magnetic compass that directed Renaissance explorers to Asia and the Americas was discovered in the twelfth century.

The Forces of Change

But the medieval society that stood on the brink of Renaissance in 1300 was a society in trouble. As the historian Charles G. Nauert comments:

> Medieval civilization contained some fundamental defects. . . . The crisis that became evident in the fourteenth century has been compared to the crisis that shattered [ancient] Roman society. . . . [Unlike Rome,] European civilization survived . . . because it was flexible enough to make fundamental modifications.[1]

Feudalism, the medieval social order, no longer worked. It had developed at a

Michelangelo's statue David *remains one of the great works of art to come out of the Renaissance.*

The Catholic Church had also provided stability to medieval society. However, the late medieval church was suffering from its own problems. Many in the clergy had used their position to build political power and personal fortunes. The pope had fallen under the control of the king of France and would not win free of this influence until the last quarter of the fourteenth century. Because of these and other problems, the church had become a more disruptive than constructive social force.

Other forces were also at work altering the medieval way of life. The economy was changing because of an increase in trade, which had begun with the Crusades. Returning crusaders had introduced Europe to spices, silks, and other luxuries found in the Near East. The growing trade sparked interest in other parts of the world, and what had once been a closed society began to open up and expand.

Responding to Change and Opportunity

time when the economy of Europe was based on agriculture and political power rested in the hands of the local nobility. However, late medieval society was more complex, and feudalism was inadequate to meet the demands of this new era. Among other things, it had no provisions for dealing with the towns and cities that had grown up in the last centuries of the Middle Ages. Nor did its loose political structure provide the means to build and run countries with strong central governments, which were beginning to take shape in England and France.

The transition from medieval to Renaissance society came about because the people of Europe developed new ways of doing many things. And in the doing, the Renaissance crackled with energy. As Europeans looked around them, they saw activity everywhere. Trade and industry were booming. Explorers were establishing sea routes to distant Asia and discovering new lands in the Americas. Scholars were founding libraries and filling them with unearthed ancient manuscripts and with newly written books, many detailing recent scientific discoveries in such fields as astronomy and anatomy. Artists and sculptors were producing great works in paint and stone.

To Europeans, this time of the Renaissance was a new age, filled with awesome accomplishments. Many would have agreed with the French physician Jean Fernel, who wrote in the early 1500s:

> The world sailed round, the largest of Earth's continents discovered, . . . the printing press sowing knowledge, gunpowder revolutionizing the art of war, ancient manuscripts rescued. . . , all witness to the triumph of our New Age.[2]

The many accomplishments of the society were also mirrored in the varied interests and achievements of specific individuals.

For instance, the anonymous biographer of the fifteenth-century Italian Leon Battista Alberti says that Alberti, who thought of himself as an architect, also "taught himself music. . . . He took up civil law for some years. . . . At the age of twenty-four he turned to physics and mathematics."[3] Others, such as Leonardo da Vinci, would be as versatile, giving rise to the term "Renaissance man."

In science, in art, in government, and in finance, creativity dominated the Renaissance. For, as the historian Robert Ergang writes, "the age of the Renaissance is one of the great creative periods of history. . . . [It] was . . . a time which gave new direction to intellectual endeavor . . . leading to . . . modern civilization."[4]

1 Humanists and Culture

The fifteenth century saw one of the greatest scavenger hunts in history. All over Europe and the Near East, eager searchers ransacked the dusty shelves of monasteries and old public buildings. Stashed away in these places were treasures—not gold and silver but ancient Greek and Roman manuscripts. As a result of this search, the surviving writings of such classical authors as Plato, Sophocles, Cicero, and Plutarch came into Renaissance hands. The searchers, financed by princes, merchants, and other rich individuals, did their work well; by 1500, they had unearthed almost all the ancient writings in existence today.

The powerful and wealthy collectors of these manuscripts built libraries to house their growing collections, libraries that drew those interested in learning as much as possible about the great people, ideas, and art of antiquity. This learning would shape the development of the Renaissance.

The New Learning

During the Renaissance, the study of classical works was known as the New Learning. In time, however, this revival of interest in classical letters and the value of the indi-vidual became known as humanism because its practitioners were concerned first and foremost with human affairs, as opposed to the spiritual or divine.

However, although humanism emphasized and focused on humanity, its followers did not deny the existence of God, nor did they see any conflict between humanism and Christianity. Indeed, many leading Renaissance humanists belonged to the clergy of the Catholic Church. To the humanists, God was a given from which "they proceeded to investigate man, his capacities, his deeds, and his accomplishments."[5]

The Rise of Humanism

As was the Renaissance itself, humanism was born in Italy. Two major factors sparked the mania for classical study that swept fourteenth- and fifteenth-century Italy. First, surrounded as they were by the ruins of the Roman Empire, Italian scholars found intriguing source material close at hand, sparking a fascination with their past that led to the search for more surviving Roman writings.

Second, the influx of refugees from the crumbling Byzantine Empire created a growing interest in classical Greece. The Byzantine Empire was descended from the eastern half of the old Roman Empire, which operated throughout the Middle Ages. Centered on the Balkan Peninsula, the empire's official language was Greek, and its libraries contained many Greek works that had disappeared in the west.

In the fourteenth century, the Ottoman Turks invaded and eventually conquered the Byzantine Empire with the capture of the imperial capital of Constantinople in 1453. Many Byzantines fleeing the Turks sought safety in the west. Armed with copies of original Greek manuscripts, these refugees set themselves up as Greek scholars and teachers. The historian Will

Durant observes that "Greek [Byzantine] professors . . . left Constantinople . . . and served as carriers of the classic germ; so year by year Italy rediscovered Greece."[6]

A New Technology

A contributing factor to the spread of humanism was printing. Until the Renaissance, books were produced by hand, each volume individually copied and bound. Then, around 1450, the printing press was invented in Germany, with many historians giving the credit to Johannes Gutenberg.

The interior of a seventeenth-century printing shop. The invention of the printing press eliminated the laborious process of copying books by hand and thus accelerated the spread of literature.

Although printing technology had been developed in China as early as the second century A.D., the mechanism was a clumsy affair of hand-carved wooden letters, which generally produced poor quality print. However, the fifteenth-century printing press was combined with another innovation: movable metal type (perhaps another Gutenberg invention). This combination turned out pages with sharp, clear letters.

The Rise of Literacy

Even though books could now be more easily produced and distributed, early printed volumes were large, bulky, and expensive, affordable only to wealthy individuals. However, by the end of the fifteenth century, the introduction of smaller type sizes made for smaller, inexpensive books. Suddenly, books, some in pocket-size editions that people could carry around with them, became available to everyone, significantly speeding up the spread of classical knowledge and humanist ideas.

And who was reading about ancient lore and humanist concepts in these newly printed works? Whereas in the Middle Ages only the clergy and a few others could read, Renaissance readers came from all social classes and walks of life. They included, of course, scholars and students but also aristocrats, merchants, and tradespeople. They numbered among them both men and women. Indeed, by the middle of the sixteenth century, about half the population of London could read and write to some degree; other European cities had similar literacy rates.

By making books plentiful and easily affordable, the printing press certainly led more people to reading and writing. However, even before the advent of the press, literacy was on the rise in Europe. The aristocracy saw literacy as a civilizing influence, and those who could read and write generally advanced further at court. The nascent middle class found literacy a valuable tool in running a business, which required written records and reports. Beginning in the late fifteenth century, guilds, professional trade organizations, required that apprentices be able to read and write.

Literacy was for the most part a city trait, with few in the country, aside from the aristocracy, learning to read, since it was not yet essential for farming. Still, most rural villages had at least one reader who would read aloud to the community from books bought from traveling booksellers.

The Spread of Education

This desire and need for reading and writing prompted the growth of schools. Elementary schools popped up all over Europe, attended by both boys and girls. These schools taught reading, writing, arithmetic, history, geography, and religion. The boys, if their parents so desired, could receive advanced education, which included Latin, philosophy, and law, at secondary schools and universities. Girls were occasionally instructed in these subjects by private tutors.

Formal schooling was mostly confined to the middle class. The nobility generally taught their children at home, while the poor, laborers and peasants, often did not go to school at all because they could not afford the fees. However, they sometimes attended charity schools run by the church.

The Father of Humanism

From this growing body of students and graduates came the scholars who created and promoted humanism. Among the first of the humanists was the Italian Francesco Petrarca, better known as Petrarch, an enthusiastic and untiring collector and promoter of classical literature. Born in 1304,

Petrarch studied and preserved many of the largely forgotten works of the ancient Romans and Greeks.

he was supported by a series of wealthy sponsors, or patrons, and thus was able to devote his life to studying and writing about antiquity. Before Petrarch's death in 1374, historian Crane Brinton writes that

> he assembled a splendid private library and found in an Italian cathedral some dusty and forgotten letters of [Roman statesman] Cicero which threw new light on that Roman's political career. Petrarch so admired the past that he addressed a series of affectionate letters to Cicero and other old masters and composed a Latin epic in the manner of the Aeneid. . . . Although he never learned Greek well enough to read it, he could at least gaze reverently at his manuscripts of Homer and Plato.[7]

Although today Petrarch is best known for his sonnets written in Italian, in his own day, he and others considered his writings in Latin to be his most important work. In recognition of his literary accomplishments, the senate of Rome crowned Petrarch poet laureate in 1341.

Reading the Past

Petrarch was not alone in his inability to read Greek; few early humanists could. Reading Latin manuscripts posed no serious problems because Latin had been used throughout western Europe during the Middle Ages by the Catholic Church and by medieval scholars. Such was not the case with Greek, however; with rare exceptions, Greek had not been spoken or written in the west for centuries. Not until the close of the fourteenth century did humanists begin to learn the language. Even

Petrarch Writes to Cicero

In the following 1345 letter, taken from his Letters of Old Age *and supposedly addressed to Cicero, the Italian humanist Petrarch explains why he so admires the Roman statesman.*

"Francesco [Petrarch] sends his greetings to Cicero. . . . Allow me to say, O Cicero, that you lived as a man, you spoke as an orator [speaker], you wrote as a philosopher. . . . I applaud your talent and your eloquence, . . . not I alone but all who bedeck [cover] themselves with the flowers of Latin speech are grateful to you; for it is with the waters from your wellsprings that we irrigate our fields, frankly admitting that we are sustained [supported] by your leadership, aided by your judgments, and enlightened by your radiance. . . . Under your auspices [sponsorship], . . . we have achieved whatever writing skills and principles that we possess. . . .

About your books, . . . some splendid volumes still exist. . . ; your works enjoy an immense reputation and your name is on everyone's lips. . . . Some of your books, I suspect, are lost for us who still live, and I know not whether they will ever be recovered: how great is my grief, how great a shame for our times, how great a wrong to posterity! . . . And furthermore, even of the surviving books, large portions are missing; it is though after winning a great battle . . . , we now have to mourn our leaders, and not only those who have been killed but those who have been maimed or lost."

then, Renaissance Europeans often preferred to read ancient Greek works in Latin translations.

The humanists soon noticed that differences existed between ancient and medieval Latin, and they began to view the medieval version as a corrupt form of the language. Many purist Renaissance scholars demanded a return to the eloquence they believed only classical Latin possessed. In 1444, Lorenzo Valla (1407–1457) argued for a rigid adherence to the rules of ancient Latin in *De Elegantiae linguae latinae (The Elegances of the Latin Language)*. Valla's work proved to be very popular with humanist scholars, and *De Elegantiae linguae latinae* helped to create a whole corps of intellectuals, whose chief goal in life was to work out the rules for classical Latin grammar.

Valla's book also found an audience outside of scholars. Many middle-class merchants, for instance, could read Latin since it was considered necessary for communicating with foreign businesses, and

Lorenzo Valla on Latin

Italian humanist Lorenzo Valla's influential 1444 The Elegances of the Latin Language *argues that Latin is the most important legacy of the classical world. The following excerpt is found in Donald R. Kelley's* Renaissance Humanism.

"When I consider . . . the deeds of our ancestors [the Romans]. . . , ours seem to me to have excelled all others not only in empire but even in the propagation [spread] of their language. . . . For no people has spread its language so far as ours has done, who in a short space of time has made the Roman tongue . . . almost throughout the entire West and not a negligible [small] part of the North and Africa. . . .

The Roman dominion [rule], the peoples and nations long ago threw off as an unwelcome burden; the language of Rome they have thought sweeter than any nectar, more splendid than any silk, more precious than any gold or gems, and they have embraced it as if it were a god sent from Paradise. Great, therefore, . . . is the . . . power of the Latin language, truly great in its divinity, which has been preserved these many centuries with religion and holy awe. . . . We have lost Rome, we have lost authority. . . , yet we reign [rule] still. . . . For wherever the Roman tongue holds sway, there is the Roman Empire.

Who does not know that when the Latin language flourishes, all studies and disciplines thrive, as they are ruined when it perishes? For whom have been the most profound [serious] philosophers, the best orators [speakers], . . . and the greatest writers but those indeed who have been most zealous [enthusiastic] in speaking well [in Latin]."

thus they were interested in improving their use of the language.

The Donation of Constantine

Lorenzo Valla had many other interests besides Latin. Opinionated and intolerant, he savagely attacked the ideas of other humanists, such as the claim that emotions could be controlled through reason. Valla also supported the unpopular position that moderate pleasure made for a good life, not a sinful one, and he offended many humanists by criticizing Cicero's Latin, which he, unlike his fellow scholars, felt was grammatically flawed.

Besides his work on Latin, Valla was most famous for his analysis of a document called the Donation of Constantine. The Donation was supposedly a grant from the fourth-century Roman emperor Constantine giving the pope authority over secular, or nonreligious, rulers. Valla took a hard, critical look at this document when Pope Eugenius IV used it to challenge the claim of Alfonso I, Valla's employer, to the throne of Naples.

By comparing this document with classical works from Constantine's period, Valla was able to show that both the Latin used and the historical references made were from a time centuries after Constantine's death. His conclusions were so convincing that the Donation of Constantine was utterly discredited, thus ending the pope's claimed authority over Alfonso and other rulers. By showing that the Donation of Constantine was a forgery, Valla had extended the power of humanism beyond the study walls.

Patrons and the Medici

The spread of humanism in Italy, and later throughout Europe, was aided by wealthy patrons. In the northern Italian city-state of Milan, for instance, the ruling Visconti and Sforza families were enthusiastic humanists, supporting many teachers, artists, and philosophers. The Visconti were Petrarch's patrons for a time, and the Sforza sponsored Constantine Lascaris, who produced the first book in Greek published in Renaissance Italy.

However, it was farther south, in Florence, that humanism found its most zealous patrons, the Medici. Perhaps the richest family in Renaissance Italy, the Medici earned their fortune as successful bankers and traders. Their wealth eventually bought them political control of Florence, which they turned into one of the great cultural centers of the Renaissance.

Cosimo de' Medici (1389–1464), who ruled Florence from 1434 to his death, for example, established the first public library in Italy, supported numerous artists and writers, and encouraged the study of Greek. Cosimo's library, open free of charge to teachers and students, was filled with thousands of ancient manuscripts. Many of these works were originals, scavenged by Medici agents from Greece and Egypt, often at great cost to Cosimo. The

Lorenzo de' Medici was a tyrannical ruler but also a patron of the arts who favored education.

remainder were copies made by a permanent staff of forty-five scribes, again supported by Medici money.

Cosimo's powerful grandson Lorenzo (1449–1492), the tyrant of Florence from 1469 to 1492, was an even more generous patron than his grandfather. Known as the Magnificent, Lorenzo was himself a scholar, schooled in both philosophy and Greek. He expanded his grandfather's manuscript collection, once saying that he wished he could spend his entire fortune on the purchase of books. He also took an active part in the debates of the humanists with whom he surrounded himself. As his contemporary the Italian political writer Niccolò Machiavelli observed,

> [Lorenzo] loved exceedingly all who excelled in the arts, and he showered favors on the learned. . . . To give the youth of Florence an opportunity of studying letters he founded a college at Pisa [then under Florentine control], to which he had appointed the most excellent professors that Italy could produce. . . . In his conversation he was ready and eloquent. . . . There had never died in Florence . . . one . . . who left behind him so wide a reputation for wisdom.[8]

The Platonic Academy

In 1439, Cosimo de' Medici organized and financed the Platonic Academy, which promoted study of the classics. Under Lorenzo, the Academy became one of the most important intellectual centers in Italy. Similar humanist clubs would spring up all over Italy and Europe, and many

Renaissance humanists admired the works of the Greek philosopher Plato, in part because his ideas did not conflict with Christian theology.

played important roles in the development of Renaissance thought, art, and science.

These Renaissance associations were modeled on the ancient Greek philosopher Plato's Academy, in which teachers and students met to discuss and debate philosophical issues, such as the nature of knowledge, love, and death. Plato was a revered figure during the Renaissance, his popular appeal based on his belief that values, or as he called them "ideas," were absolute and unchanging. Plato's belief in absolute ideas fit nicely with Christian theology, particularly his insistence that all earthly things were created and given shape by the highest of these ideas, which Plato labeled the Supreme Form of the Good. The humanist Marsilio Ficino describes the Good as the "one wise intelligence in command, the leader of all things, which can give a beginning to everything and establish an end."[9] It was an easy step for Christians to conclude that this Good was God.

Florence's Platonic Academy saw as its special mission the squaring of Platonic thought, as well as classical philosophy in general, with Christianity. The Academy was not the first to be interested in this matter. Petrarch, in the previous century, had sought to create a stronger brand of Christianity by wedding the teachings of St. Augustine with the philosophy of Cicero.

The Humanists of Florence

A number of famous humanists were members of the Platonic Academy. Marsilio Ficino (1433–1499), who became the head of the Academy, produced a 1483 Latin translation of Plato's work that helped popularize the Greek philosopher throughout Renaissance Europe and remained in print through the next century. Angelo Ambrogini, better known as Politian, was an early expert on Greek writers, and his Latin translation of the *Iliad* made Homer's work available to those who did not read Greek.

Ficino's nephew, Giovanni Pico della Mirandola (1463–1494), was perhaps the most accomplished of all the group's members, fluent not only in Latin and Greek but also in Hebrew and Arabic. Reading widely in works written in all these languages, he sought a common factor that would unite all religions, ancient and modern. Although he failed to find that factor, he did found the disciplines of comparative religion and comparative philosophy.

In 1486, in an attempt to find his common religious denominator, Pico proposed nine hundred theses, or questions, for a debate to be held in Rome. Pico even promised to pay the way of anyone who was interested in taking part but too poor to travel.

However, the debate never took place because the pope at the time, Innocent VIII, ruled that some of the theses smacked of heresy, opinions contrary to the Catholic Church's teachings. Pico defended himself against this charge in 1486 in *De hominis dignitate oratio (Oration on the Dignity of Man)*, which the historian Samuel Dresden describes as "*the* manifesto . . . of humanism." In the *Oratio*, Pico defends the human focus of humanism when he says, "I have read in Arabian books that nothing in the world can be found that is more worthy of admiration than man."[10]

Humanism and the Universities

By no means was humanism confined to Italy. In France, Guillaume Budé (1468–1540) was recognized as one of the leading scholars of his day. He wrote important books on Roman law and the study of the Greek language. In the latter, his 1529 *Commentarii linguae Graecae (Commentaries on the Greek Language)*, he conveyed his deep enthusiasm for a language that he did not even learn until he was twenty-six. (Supposedly he was so absorbed in his Greek studies that he forgot his own wedding.)

Like other humanists, Budé was a firm believer in the importance of an education strong in the classics, and he got involved

University students, depicted here in sixteenth-century France, received a classical education drawing on a wide range of topics.

in educational reform at the university level. In 1530, while serving as court librarian for the French king, Francis I, Budé helped establish one of the first humanist universities, the College of France. Unlike older European universities, such as the Sorbonne in Paris, lectures at the College of France were given not just in Latin but also in Greek and Hebrew, and courses covered a wider range of classical learning. Students in other Renaissance universities followed the medieval practice of taking only those classes relevant to their chosen area of study. This professional, specialized education prepared a student to be a priest, doctor, or lawyer.

Humanists such as Budé rejected this tightly focused university education. Instead, influenced by the ideas of Cicero, they favored a more general, wide-ranging

education, which would expose the student to "the infinite variety of human experience"[11] through a thorough reading of both Greek and Roman literature. The humanists felt that such a general education would develop all of a student's capabilities. Also, it was Budé's and others' belief that, when combined with Christian teaching, a general classical education built character because it exposed students to many examples of heroic and moral behavior described by the ancients.

The Prince of Humanists

The most famous of all humanists was also a northern European and a contemporary of Guillaume Budé. Desiderius

Erasmus, born illegitimate in 1466 in the Netherlands, became known as the prince of humanists because he dominated the intellectual world of his day until his death in 1536.

Erasmus's early education owed little to humanism, as the Italian Renaissance had yet to influence northern European schools to any great extent. In 1487 he became a monk but left the monastery after a

The Need for a Humanistic Education

In the following 1518 letter, included in Renaissance Letters, *edited by Robert J. Clements and Lorna Levant, the English humanist Sir Thomas More explains to the faculty of Oxford University the value of humanism in religious education.*

"As to the question of humanistic education being secular. No one has ever claimed that a man needed Greek or Latin, or indeed any education in order to be saved. Still, the education which he calls secular does train the soul in virtue. . . . Even if men come . . . to study theology [religion], they do not start with that discipline. They must first study the laws of human nature and conduct, a thing not useless to theologians; without such study they might possibly preach a sermon acceptable to an academic group, without they would certainly fail to reach the common man. And from whom should they acquire such skill better than from the poets, orators [speakers], and historians [of the classical world].

Moreover, there are some who through knowledge of things natural . . . construct a ladder, by which to rise in the contemplation of things supernatural; they build a path to theology through philosophy and the liberal arts. . . .

To whom is it *not* obvious that to the Greeks we owe our precision in the liberal arts generally and theology particularly; for the Greeks either made the great discoveries themselves or passed them as part of their heritage. . . . All the Doctors [theologians] of the Latin [Catholic Church] . . . gave themselves to learning Greek."

English statesman and author Sir Thomas More believed theology students could benefit from the study of human nature.

few years to study theology in Paris. Bored and uninspired by his course work, he began tutoring other students and reading classical literature.

Then in 1499, at the age of thirty-three, Erasmus followed one of his pupils to England and there met an English humanist, John Colet of Oxford. Colet so inspired Erasmus that the Dutch monk plunged into a study of Greek to turn himself into a humanist scholar. Within a few years, Erasmus had achieved his goal, launching a career that would make him the most important humanist in Europe by the time of his death in 1536.

Over the next thirty years, Erasmus taught and lived all over western Europe, studying and teaching in not only France and England but also Italy, Germany, and

A devoted scholar of ancient Greek texts, the Dutch philosopher Erasmus became one of the most celebrated humanists of the sixteenth century.

Switzerland. He wrote thousands of letters to other important people of his day and turned out major humanist works, such as the satirical *Encomium moriae (The Praise of Folly)* (1509).

Erasmus was one of the first best-selling European writers. His work appealed to the growing reading public of the time, and the printing press made his work available to these readers. *The Praise of Folly,* for example, became an instant best-seller, going through forty-two editions of a thousand copies each during the author's lifetime. Only the Bible sold more copies.

Christian Humanism

In all his writings, Erasmus championed the basic humanist principles. He believed in human dignity and worth; he felt the values of antiquity were harmonious with those of Christian Europe; and he found in the lives of certain ancients, such as Cicero and Socrates, examples of upright and moral behavior.

Erasmus's brand of humanism, however, differed somewhat from that of the south. Like many other northern humanists, among them Guillaume Budé, the Dutch monk was deeply concerned with a need to reform the Catholic Church. Although calls for church reform were heard in southern Europe, it was the northern humanists who took the lead in this campaign, and this aspect of northern humanism came to be called "Christian humanism." As historian Charles G. Nauert observes, "*Christian humanism* is often applied to . . . that part of the Northern Humanist movement that made reform of the Church the principal focus."[12]

In 1504, Erasmus wrote in his *Enchiridion militis Christiani (Handbook of the Christian Soldier)* that the Catholic Church needed to return to the simplicity of the early church and to follow more closely the teachings of the early Christian leaders. Later, in several key sections of *The Praise of Folly,* the Dutch humanist ridiculed the excesses and weaknesses of the Catholic clergy.

The Need for Church Reform

Erasmus and other critics of the Catholic Church believed that the institution had become too worldly and no longer served the spiritual needs of its members. They pointed out that illiterate and poorly trained priests were all too often unfit to tend to minister their congregations. High-ranking church officials, including the bishops and the pope himself, were attacked as being more interested in secular politics than in church matters. And indeed, Renaissance bishops often were deeply involved in local and national politics, some holding important government posts.

The popes of the time often acted more like secular rulers than spiritual leaders. For instance, Alexander VI, pope from 1492 to 1503, accused in his time of being a devil and a monster, assisted the political ambitions of his illegitimate son, Cesare Borgia, by diverting church money for Cesare's use. Alexander also helped the French invade northern Italy in exchange for Cesare's being named a duke by the French king. A later pope, Julius II, presiding from 1503 to 1513, put on armor and led the Vatican armies on a number of campaigns, conquering several neighboring cities of Rome. Such acts led the Italian historian Francesco Guicciardini to write in his 1561 *Storia d'Italia (History of Italy):*

> Having obtained temporal [worldly] power . . . , they [the popes] . . . forgot divine commands and the salvation of their souls. . . . Their aim was no longer a holy life; no longer the spread of Christianity; no longer doing good to their neighbor. They became interested in armies, . . . the accumulation of treasure, new laws, new methods . . . to draw money from every side.[13]

The Goals of the Reformers

Many of those calling for reform, in particular Erasmus, Budé, and the English humanist Thomas More, wanted to correct the church from within. Others, however, found more radical solutions. In October 1517, a German humanist and professor of theology, Martin Luther (1483–1546), directly challenged church authority. He drew up ninety-five theses, which detailed church practices that Luther felt led to abuse, corruption, and a weakening of faith.

Four years later, Luther's confrontation with the Catholic Church led to his excommunication, that is, expulsion from the church. By then, however, his actions had launched the Reformation, which would give rise to Protestantism as other northern humanists, such as the Frenchman John Calvin and the English king Henry VIII, also broke with the Catholic

Martin Luther nails his ninety-five theses to the door of the Castle Church in Wittenberg. Luther's complaints against the Catholic Church's abuses of power led to the Reformation and the creation of the Protestant faith.

Church. The last century of the Renaissance would be marked by increasingly fierce religious persecution and war as Catholics and Protestants fought each other over their differing beliefs.

Humanism's influence on aspects of Renaissance culture other than religion were equally great, though generally less dramatic. As the scholar John Hale points out:

> By the early sixteenth century the influence of classical scholarship, and its popularization through translations . . . , had acquired a critical mass which produced unstoppable chain reactions. There was hardly a branch of inquiry, from jurisprudence [law] to mathematics, military science, and the arts, that was unaltered by . . . a relevant text, artefact, or record of historical experience.[14]

Even business and politics, human activities generally not associated with scholarship, were affected by the rise of humanism during the Renaissance.

2 Merchants and Commerce

The Renaissance was an age of flourishing commerce, and Europe in general was rich. Wealth flowed from all sorts of businesses, with fortunes made in trading, manufacturing, and banking. The size of some Renaissance businesses, a number of which were international concerns, and the amounts of money brought in led to the development of financial practices that are still in use in the present day.

Renaissance Society

The society that was enjoying this booming economy was divided into three classes: the upper, or ruling, class; the middle, or business, class; and the lower, or working, class. The nobility of the upper class still held much of the political power, and many owned vast estates, on which lived and worked the majority of the European population.

The workers on these estates were either free peasants or serfs, farmers bound to the land that they worked. In western Europe, however, serfdom was on its way out by the beginning of the Renaissance and had disappeared completely by its end. In eastern Europe and Russia, serfs remained common for several more cen-

turies. In all parts of Europe, few of the free peasants owned their own farms; rather, they paid rent to the estate owner, their landlord.

The crops from these estates were sold in nearby towns, which were the home of the fastest growing segment of Renaissance Europeans—the middle class. The

A frightened peasant couple embraces. During the Renaissance, peasants still represented the lowest class and were subject to abuse and taxation by their landlords.

members of the middle class were prosperous, supporting themselves through trade, the production of such goods as clothing and tools, and the handling of money.

Up and Down the Social Ladder

Mobility between the classes was possible; indeed, the middle class gained recruits from those of the working class who made their way to the towns in search of work. Many of these immigrants became lower-class laborers, but a few started businesses or learned trades that allowed them and their children to rise into the middle class.

Many wealthy Renaissance citizens took pride in their ability to purchase fine spices and luxurious cloth sold in the city markets.

And, rarely, a few of the middle class were elevated through wealth or marriage into the nobility.

Downward movement was also a possibility. Financial disaster could hurl a middle-class family into the lower class. Money problems could also send members of the aristocracy into a downward spiral. Nobles who mismanaged their estates or spent more than their income could find themselves facing poverty. Some debt-ridden aristocrats married into wealthy middle-class families, trading the prestige of their titles for money. Sometimes, such marriages dragged the nobility into the business class. Other poverty-stricken nobles who could not, or would not, partner themselves with the middle class sank all the way down to the bottom of the social ladder, scornfully called barefoot gentry by the rest of society.

Humanism on Wealth

Much of the wealth of Renaissance Europe was in the hands of the middle or business class. In general, wealthy Renaissance Europeans enjoyed their prosperity, openly boasting of the luxuries they could afford to buy. This outspoken materialism was in marked contrast to traditional Christian teachings, which still held that virtue came from self-denial and poverty. Many Renaissance Europeans, however, rejected the idea that virtue was tied to poverty. They saw nothing wrong with being rich and with showy displays of wealth in the form of expensive wardrobes, furnishings, and art.

This Renaissance materialism was strongly supported by a number of humanists. The Italian humanist Poggio Bracci-

Philosophy and Money

Many humanists saw nothing wrong with wealth, and indeed, some even thought it acceptable for philosophers and writers to prosper, as can be seen in the following 1362 letter by Petrarch, taken from his Letters on Familiar Matters.

"Those who seek . . . out [wealth] . . . should not . . . be blamed, provided they take care in their zeal for possessions not to overlook justice, moderation, compassion, and decency. . . . In *De Office,* . . . [Cicero] says, 'An enhancement of one's property that harms no one must not be condemned, but wrong-doing must always be avoided.' . . . [The Roman statesman Seneca] says. . . , 'Stop forbidding money to philosophers. No one has condemned wisdom to poverty.' . . .

Plato and Aristotle were no more renowned . . . before they sought or accepted money than afterward. . . . I am aware that a base [bad] or relentless quest for wealth does harm to famous names, although not the honorable possession of enormous wealth. Was [the Roman poet] Virgil less distinguished after . . . gold made him wealthy than when he headed for Rome, a poor exile. . . . In general, nothing can budge a spirit well based and firmly rooted. . . .

I would certainly rather be rich than poor. . . . Nothing is more vexing than extreme want. . . . Riches must not be . . . rejected too haughtily. . . . It is not ambition nor even cupidity [greed] to accept happily . . . the gifts . . . of God."

olini wrote in his 1428 *De avarita (Of Avarice)* that wanting money and property served a useful social role because it made people work. Other humanists believed that the desire for money was a normal part of human nature and that trade and money were essential in building and maintaining civilization. As historian Ernst Breisach notes,

Some humanists gave powerful support to . . . economic activities and . . .

the accumulation of wealth. A good example is the humanist answer to the traditional call of purists for poverty as the ideal Christian condition. Far from condemning the possession of property many humanists . . . emphasized the increased opportunities for being virtuous which became available to those of means. [The fifteenth-century humanist] Leon Battista Alberti . . . stated that man needs a home, property, and a job to be fully a man.[15]

In Praise of Wealth

The Italian humanist Leonardo Bruni argues in support of Renaissance materialism and consumption in his notes to his translation of Aristotle's Economics, *published in 1445, the year after Bruni's death. This excerpt is reprinted in* The Humanism of Leonardo Bruni.

"He [Aristotle] says that the head of the household must . . . be . . . the kind of man who will be quick and skillful at making a profit. . . . This, then, is a talent that the head of the household should possess above all others, that is making a profit from the fruits of his estates and other business. . . .

He [the head of the household] should moreover be the sort . . . [who knows] how to make his wealth an adornment, and to enjoy it. . . . Not that it is seemly to make ourselves its [wealth's] slaves, . . . but to turn it to our service. Wealth will lend adornment and honor . . . if we make our outlays opportunely [spending wisely] and gracefully. These will include building a house in keeping with our wealth, having a good staff of servants, sufficient furniture, a decent array [collection] of horses and clothing. They will also include generosity to friends and patronage of public events, such as circus games . . . and public banquets, all of which should be in proportion and keeping with the man's wealth.

We shall enjoy our wealth if we take from it our sustenance [nourishment] and convenience. For we should not be so abstemious [restrained] of the goods we have acquired as to go without in the midst of plenty."

Critics of Commerce

Not all humanists approved of the widespread materialism of the period. Erasmus, and others of the northern Christian humanists, thought Europe was caught in the grip of pure and simple greed. In 1508 the Dutch scholar wrote that "it is against nature, as Aristotle said. . . , for money to breed money. . . . Nowadays . . . there is nothing . . . out of which profit cannot be squeezed." [16] Martin Luther went further, saying that large profits were a form of theft, with the merchant stealing from the customer. From Switzerland, John Calvin warned that to be overly concerned with money was to place one's soul in danger.

However, such opposition to commerce had little effect on Renaissance business. Indeed, Erasmus had a portrait painted that showed him wearing the clothes of a successful merchant, and the followers of Calvin eventually came to see wealth as a sign of being favored by God. All over Europe there were many opportunities to make money and plenty of people ready to seize those opportunities.

The Business of Trade

One of those major profit-making opportunities in the Renaissance was trading. Raw materials from one locale were sold for profit to manufacturers in another, and additional profits were generated by then selling the finished goods.

Despite a growing industry, the Renaissance was not a time of industrial revolution. Most European products were still hand made by individual workers, laboring either alone or in very small groups.

A few industries in the Renaissance did produce large quantities of merchandise. But this early "mass production" was still done by hand. For instance, to mass produce wool cloth required hundreds of workers weaving on hand looms. Printing was almost the only business that depended upon a machine—the printing press—and even so, the presses were hand operated.

The Merchants

Successful merchants grew more powerful as their businesses expanded, trading first with other European regions and then with the Near East, Asia, and, finally, the Americas. They bought and sold, among other things, iron, wool, wine, and spices, still common commodities in the modern world. The largest profits generally came

Master goldsmiths and their apprentices at work in sixteenth-century France. Most merchandise was crafted by hand during the Renaissance, and mass production by machine was roughly three hundred years in the future.

In Venice, the richest city in Europe, Renaissance merchants gained both wealth and political power.

from marketing such luxury items as fur and silk.

Renaissance merchants were often great travelers. According to Will Durant:

> They were seldom such businessmen as we know today, safe and sedentary behind a desk in their own city. Usually they moved with their goods, often they traveled great distances to buy cheaply . . . and returned to sell dear where their goods were rare. . . . Merchants were adventurers, explorers, knights of the caravan, armed with daggers and bribes, ready for highwaymen [robbers], pirates, and a thousand tribulations.[17]

Venice and the Mediterranean Trade

Successful merchants came to dominate both the growing middle class and local governments. However, few merchants were as politically powerful as those in the northern Italian city-state of Venice, strategically located on the Adriatic coast. Venice built a huge trading empire in the Mediterranean, dating from its role as a jumping-off place for the crusaders of the eleventh century. In the Near East, the Venetians traded western wool, lead, and tin for dyes, silk, spices, sugar, and cotton. Some of the Near Eastern trade goods were originally from Asia, imported from as far away as China along centuries-old land routes.

Commerce transformed and supported Venice's political organization. Venice had once been ruled by a doge, or duke, elected by Venetian citizens, but during the Renaissance, actual political control was in the hands of the city-state's merchants. A select group of old trading families controlled Venice as members of the Great Council, which appointed the officials who formed the government. The Great Council, instead of the Venetian citizens, now elected the doge, who became a figurehead overseeing official ceremonies and entertaining important foreign visitors.

Venice was by no means the only Italian city-state engaged in Mediterranean trade. Genoa, situated on Italy's west coast, amassed a trading empire to match that of Venice. Their rivalry for the lucrative eastern trade led first to competition for goods and markets, then to friction, and finally to war. In 1380 the Venetians emerged triumphant when they captured the Genoese fleet, a blow from which Genoa never recovered. By the beginning of the fifteenth century, as Robert Ergang observes, Venice "was the richest city in Europe with an income larger than that of [whole] kingdoms. It also had a fleet of warships larger than any other . . . [European] power."[18]

The Hanseatic League

Trade in northern Europe also boomed during the Renaissance. Unlike in the south, where luxury items such as spices

and silk brought the highest profits, in the north it was food, particularly wheat and fish, that was most valuable. Much of this trade centered on the Baltic Sea, across which wheat from the rich farmlands of northeastern Europe was shipped to England and the rest of western Europe.

The Baltic was also rich in fish. Salted herring was particularly prized because it did not spoil easily, could be shipped long distances, and was cheap. Historian Emil Lucki writes that "the catch was rich, the packing cheap because of the accessibility to abundant supplies of timber for barrels, the market close by, and the demand extensive. Profits were substantial."[19]

To control this profitable trade and to protect it from pirates and bandits, the cities of northern Germany formed in the thirteenth century a trading alliance called the Hanseatic League, which took its name from the German *Hanse,* meaning

A Venetian party is crowded with wealthy merchants and nobility. Such galas were often staged to exhibit the wealth and status of those in attendance.

This sixteenth-century woodcut illustrates the goods of a prosperous merchant. Booming trade during the Renaissance led to the rise of the merchant class.

association or company. At its height, the league numbered close to a hundred towns, led by Lübeck, Hamburg, and Daniz.

Although it had no formal government, the Hanseatic League members assembled when necessary to decide policy; apportion money for joint ventures, particularly military campaigns; make and ratify treaties; and dispatch diplomats. The league even had its own legal code and flag.

The Power of the Hansa

Much as Venice monopolized trade in the Mediterranean, so did the Hanseatic League in the Baltic Sea, acting as middleman between northeastern Europe, including Russia, and England, Scandinavia, and the Low Countries (eventually to become the Netherlands, Belgium, and Luxembourg). In addition to wheat and salted herring, the Hansa sent wax, timber, tar, pitch, furs, and copper west. To the east, it brought wool, wine, salt, and silver.

As did Venice, the league fought to keep its tight grip on its trade goods and routes. In 1370, for instance, the league fought and won a war with Denmark after the Danish king Valdemar IV had harassed Hansa shipping and then attacked a league town. The Treaty of Stralsund that ended the fighting freed the Hansa from paying Denmark's custom duties, gave it virtual control over several Danish cities for five years, and allowed it a hand in selecting the next king of Denmark.

Later, in 1406, English fishermen tried to invade the fishing grounds of the Baltic. The Hansa took swift and direct action, sending a fleet that captured almost a hundred English fishermen. The German captains then had the fishermen bound hand and foot and tossed overboard to drown.

The Hansa in Decline

Not all northern trade was in the hands of the Hanseatic League. Both England and the Low Countries had growing trade interests in Europe, although outside the Baltic. For instance, by sailing north around Scandinavia to the White Sea, English merchants opened their own trade routes to Russia. Closer to home, England exported wool to the Low Countries, which turned the wool into finished cloth for export. The Low Countries also imported iron ore from Spain.

By the fifteenth century, Hanseatic power in the Baltic was dwindling. In part, this decline was caused by a shift in fishing grounds. The herring that had up till now lived and bred in the Baltic moved for some unknown reason into the North Sea, outside of Hansa control.

However, the major cause of the league's decline was internal. Rivalries among various league towns and jealousies among the Hansa's most powerful merchants sapped Hanseatic power. Loyalty to the league ran a distant second to each member's self-interest.

The divided league was unable to cope with the rise of strong rivals, such as the kingdoms of Lithuania and Poland, as well as the union of Denmark, Sweden, and Norway. The Hansa, handicapped by its bickering members, could not respond swiftly enough to counter the moves of its better organized competitors. Finally, in the middle of the sixteenth century, the Hanseatic League was given a death blow when the Dutch grabbed away the last of the east-west Baltic trade from the Hansa.

Venice Loses Its Monopoly

Like the Hanseatic League, Venice also found itself in trouble when, in the late fifteenth century, it began to lose control of its Asian and Near Eastern trade. The Venetian monopoly began to crumble when it was blocked by the Ottoman Empire, whose rule by the late 1400s covered the entire eastern Mediterranean. Whenever possible, the Ottoman Turks hindered Venetian trading, and Venice found itself fighting a series of costly wars with the Turks.

A second and even more damaging threat to Venice was the rise of trade rivals in western Europe. Both Spain and Portugal were anxious to grab a share of the lucrative eastern trade. Blocked by both Venice and the Ottoman Empire from the eastern Mediterranean, these countries sought other ways of reaching Asia. Spain tried to find a westward sea route to China, while Portugal put its efforts into sailing around Africa to India.

During the Renaissance jobs became increasingly specialized. The sixteenth-century tailors pictured here may have been individually trained in different stages of garment making.

Industry and Manufacturing

Among the items most eagerly traded in the Renaissance were the raw materials needed to make clothing, ships, glassware, wine, beer, soap, and gunpowder. Thus, wool from England became finished cloth in the Low Countries. Glass from the Near East was turned into glassware in Venice and other Italian cities. Timber from the Baltic and the Near East provided the lumber to build the ships of trade and exploration.

The labor force in such industries became increasingly specialized: For example, for wool manufacturing, different workers took care of the material at each step of production, from washing to combing to carding, spinning, weaving, and dyeing. In Venice, the ship-building labor pool, which consisted of one thousand workers and which was ranked from unskilled to highly skilled, was so efficiently organized that, by the sixteenth century, it could turn out three completed ships every two days.

Commercial Inventions

Modern business owes more than job specialization to the Renaissance. For example, the modern corporation had its birth in the Renaissance. One of the first of these early corporations was the English Muscovy Company, founded in 1533 to trade with Russia. As do modern corporations, the Muscovy and other Renaissance corporate firms sold shares, known as stocks, to raise money for their operations.

But perhaps the most important financial instrument of the Renaissance was double-entry bookkeeping. First used in Genoa in the early fourteenth century, the practice spread to the rest of Italy and then into northern Europe. It remains today one of the essential tools of any efficient business. Lucki notes that "double-entry bookkeeping is regarded by business-

men as an indispensable method of keeping themselves posted on their financial standing, and its adoption has been interpreted as a sign of commercial maturity."[20]

Double-entry bookkeeping is important because it provides a check on the accuracy of a business's financial records. Without reliable records, an enterprise cannot determine whether it is making or losing money.

In double-entry bookkeeping, each business transaction is recorded twice, credited to one account and debited to another. A business can have many separate accounts, including among others, cash on hand, sales, outstanding loans, and the value of equipment and merchandise. A merchant who pays off a loan, for instance, first credits the payment to his account of outstanding loans and then debits it to his cash account. In double-entry bookkeeping, total credits always equal total debits. Thus, the double-entry process is a check-and-balance accounting system, and a busi-

Money changers of the Renaissance performed many of the same functions as modern bankers, including making loans and securing deposits.

The Sin of Interest

One of the objections the Catholic Church and other Christians had to banking was the charging of interest on loans, which was considered to be a sin, known as usury. In the following 1545 letter, quoted in Renaissance Letters, *the Protestant reformer John Calvin concludes that charging interest is not a sin.*

"In the first place, by no testimony of the Scriptures is usury wholly condemned. For the meaning of the saying of Christ, commonly thought to be very clear [on usury], . . . has been perverted. . . . The reasoning of Saint Ambrose . . . , that money does not beget [breed] money, is in my judgment too superficial. What does the sea beget? What does the land? I receive income from the rental of a house. Is it because the money grows there? The earth produces things from which money is made, and the use of a house can be bought for money. And is not money more fruitful in trade than any other form of possession one can mention? Is it lawful to let [rent] a farm, requiring a payment in return, and unlawful to receive any profit from the use of money? . . .

How do merchants derive [earn] their profit? By their industry, you will say. Certainly if money is shut up in a strong-box, it will be barren. . . . Whoever asks a loan of me does not intend to keep this money idle and gain nothing. The profit is not in the money itself, but in the return that comes from its use."

ness employing it and maintaining accurate balanced accounts can trust its financial records and rely on any calculations based on them.

The Rise of Banking

Out of the Renaissance also came the modern bank. The banks of the period grew out of coin exchanges, which were needed because the great trading centers, such as Venice and the Hanseatic League, brought in not only goods from other parts of Europe but also foreign currency. More than two hundred currencies floated through Europe during the Renaissance, and few merchants could keep track of relative rates of exchange, preferring to consult experts at the coin exchanges.

Coin exchanging became true banking in the modern sense with the acceptance and safeguarding of deposits and the issuance of loans for profit. These Renaissance banks also offered another important service now common to modern banks: They arranged for funds to be transferred from different regions. The bankers of the time did many of these transfers on paper, thus reducing the need to ship actual money from place to place.

The Bankers of Florence

During the early Renaissance, the most important bankers, called the Lombard bankers, were located in northern Italy. The center of this Lombard banking industry was Florence, with its eighty great financial houses. Most of these Florentine firms were located on a single street called Evil Street, not because of the banks' reputations but because the street had once been the haunt of murderers and thieves. The banks of Florence soon opened branches in other parts of Italy and Europe. The Medici firm alone established sixteen branches during the fifteenth century.

One of the richest men of the Renaissance, Jakob Fugger was also a philanthropist who shared his extensive wealth with the poor.

At its height, Florence was richer than the largest kingdoms of Renaissance Europe. Its gold florin became an international coin good anywhere in Europe or the Near East. The florin financed not only Renaissance businesses but also the operations of the Catholic Church and the wars of various European countries. Durant observes:

> The eighty banking houses of Florence . . . invested the savings of their depositors. They cashed checks . . . , issued letters of credit . . . , exchanged merchandise as well as credit, and supplied governments with funds for peace and war. . . . Florence became the financial capital of Europe from the thirteenth through the fifteenth century; it was there that the rates of exchange were fixed for the currencies of Europe.[21]

The Fuggers

The fifteenth century saw the establishment of the first non-Italian banking firms, such as the first Spanish bank in Barcelona in 1401. The most successful of these non-Italian banks was owned and run by the Fuggers, a German family operating out of Augsburg, in southern Bavaria. The Fuggers first became prosperous selling cloth. Then, in the 1450s, they began expanding their line of trade goods and also moved into banking.

The family's fortunes exploded in the late fifteenth and early sixteenth centuries under the guidance of Jakob Fugger (1459–1525), known as the Rich. Jakob thoroughly studied Renaissance business practices until he was an expert in bookkeeping, manufacturing, merchandising, and financing.

With these business skills, Jakob built a financial empire that stretched from Asia to the Americas, leading one unsigned, nameless contemporary to comment that "the name of Jakob Fugger and of his nephews are known in all the kingdoms and countries and even in pagan [non-European] lands. Emperors, kings, princes and nobles have sent ambassadors to them." [22]

The Fugger wealth derived not only from banking but also from mining, trading, and manufacturing. There was a Fugger express delivery service and a Fugger private postal system. By the time of Jakob Fugger's death in 1525, the firm's assets had increased tenfold. And all of this vast wealth stayed in the family because Jakob insisted that only family members hold important positions.

As head of such a powerful firm, Jakob Fugger came to see himself as a special breed of man, far superior to the ordinary person. Writing his own epitaph for his tomb, he said: "He was not comparable with anyone in his lifetime, even after death not to be counted among the mortals." He not only took pride in his exceptional wealth but also "in generosity . . . and greatness of soul." [23] To show the latter, he built a village of over a hundred houses for the poor of Augsburg. Such generosity was common among the merchant princes of the Renaissance, with many earmarking a certain percentage of their income to charity.

The Fuggers and the Habsburgs

Much of the Fuggers' wealth came from their business relations with the Habsburgs, the European royal family who ruled the Holy Roman Empire, Austria, Hungary, and for a time Spain and the Low Countries. The Habsburgs, like most other royals in Europe, were better at spending money than in making it. They were always strapped for cash to pay for their various ventures, from wars with France and England to exploration and exploitation of Mexico and South America. As a result, they borrowed money from the Fuggers to meet their payrolls.

As security for these loans, the Habsburgs gave the Fuggers control of both large estates and of gold, silver, and iron mines. For instance, in 1488, Jakob Fugger lent a large sum to Archduke Sigismund of Austria, and in exchange, he received the entire production of several silver mines until the loan was repaid.

The Fuggers were quick to take advantage of opportunity: They installed their own mine managers, who proved much more efficient than those of Sigismund, and silver production increased dramatically, as did profits. Additionally, Jakob entered into alliances with other German businesses to keep the price of silver high, thus boosting the firm's profits.

The End of the Fuggers

For a century, the Fuggers prospered from their loans to the Habsburgs, but in the late 1500s, their fortune changed. In these years, the Habsburgs fought a series of wars whose costs far exceeded their income. The Fuggers found themselves having to lend even more money in order to protect the company's already considerable investment in this royal family's affairs.

A Royal Debt

The following 1523 letter, found in Renaissance Letters, *is from Jakob Fugger to the Spanish king and Holy Roman Emperor Charles V, requesting repayment of loans owed the Fugger firm. Fugger reminds Charles that he helped pay for the latter's election to the post of emperor (Jakob personally covered over half the expenses).*

"Your Royal Majesty is undoubtedly well aware of the extent to which I and my nephews have always been inclined to serve the House of Austria [Habsburgs], and . . . to promote its welfare and its rise. For that reason, we cooperated with the former Emperor Maximilian . . . , and, in loving subjection of His Majesty, to secure the Imperial Crown for Your Imperial Majesty. . . . We also, when Your Imperial Majesty's appointed delegates were treating for the above-mentioned undertaking [election of Charles as emperor], furnished a considerable sum of money which was secured, not from me and my nephews alone, but from some of my good friends at heavy cost [borrowed at high interest]. . . .

Taking all this into consideration, my respectful request to Your Imperial Majesty is that you will graciously recognize my faithful, humble service, dedicated to the greater well-being of Your Imperial Majesty, and that you will order that the money which I have paid out, together with the interest upon it, shall be reckoned up [added up] and paid, without further delay. In order to deserve that from Your Imperial Majesty, I pledge myself to be faithful in all humility, and I hereby commend myself as faithful at all times to Your Imperial Majesty."

In the end, the Habsburgs borrowed far more than they could ever pay back. Indeed, they were not even able to keep up payment on the interest to their loans. Without the necessary funds to repay their loans, the Habsburgs simply refused to honor their debts. The result of this refusal was disastrous for the Fuggers, leading to great losses and finally bankruptcy in 1607.

The Fuggers were not the only Renaissance bankers who tied their fortunes to a European ruling family. And as the Fuggers were ruined, so were other firms when kings and princes deep in debt finally balked at repaying loans. In the interim, however, their loans, as well as the taxes and other fees businesses paid, financed the exploits of countries such as Spain, France, and England, which during the Renaissance were transformed from feudal kingdoms into modern nations.

Chapter

3 Rulers and Explorers

As Renaissance Europe was modernizing economically, it was also changing politically. Many of the loosely organized kingdoms of the Middle Ages gave way to more unified states, each headed by a strong monarch and run by a centralized government. The Renaissance saw such modern nations as Spain, France, and England take shape. As Crane Brinton observes, "We have . . . a picture [of Europe] that is not worlds apart from the present one."[24]

Leonardo Bruni and the Active Life

Humanism played an important role in the political evolution of Renaissance Europe. Although Petrarch and most other early humanists were strictly scholars and had little to do with public affairs, some later humanists took important positions as government officials. For instance, the humanist Sir Thomas More became the chief administrator for the English monarchy.

This political humanism was first promoted in the early fifteenth century by the Italian Leonardo Bruni (ca. 1370–1444), who called it "the active life." Bruni was a noted scholar of his day. His Latin translations of Aristotle, Plato, and other Greek authors made the works of these writers readily available to those who did not read Greek.

Bruni, however, was not content to study. He felt that his learning and knowledge must be applied to the world he saw around him, and he thus urged his fellow humanists to lead an active public life. Bruni took as his model the Roman statesman Cicero. To the Italian humanist, Cicero had achieved an ideal balance between scholarly and political activities and, indeed, "was the only man to have fulfilled both of these great and difficult accomplishments."[25]

Humanism and the State

Humanists were well suited to government work. Many were trained as lawyers, and all were schooled in rhetoric and languages. Nauert notes,

The arts of eloquent and persuasive speech and writing were useful to any government . . . , and so the most distinguished and successful humanists of the fifteenth and sixteenth centuries were hired to employ these arts.[26]

Even humanists who did not actually hold a government post made political contributions to their homelands by supplying models to justify the rule of strong Renaissance monarchs. They found these models in descriptions of classical Greek monarchies and in writings on the Roman Empire. Humanists also wrote histories, poems, and plays in praise of ruling families.

A number of Renaissance rulers were themselves humanists. The sixteenth century saw Francis I of France, who loved letters and the arts, open the humanist College of France. During the same century, England's Henry VIII and his daughter Elizabeth I were enthusiastic sponsors of scholarship and the arts, as well as powerful rulers intent upon consolidating political authority and funding exploration and conquest.

The Rule of Monarchs

Because emerging nations of Europe were for the most part governed by a single ruler, they became known as national monarchies. Monarchies, such as France and England, had emerged from the Middle Ages with the beginnings of central royal governments, and as the Renaissance progressed, the rulers of these countries strengthened their power base by putting more political authority in the hands of the Crown.

This consolidation of royal power was often at the expense of the aristocracy in the various regions of each kingdom. Many of these local lords had enjoyed virtual independence during the Middle Ages, but now in the Renaissance, they found themselves subject to the authority and commands of their monarch.

And that authority could be harsh. Renaissance rulers were a hard-nosed lot, acting out of ruthless self-interest. Almost all were willing to lie, cheat, steal, torture, and kill to keep and extend their individual power and authority. In 1513, the Italian Niccolò Machiavelli (1469–1527), who gave his name to the political philosophy of the age, wrote in his *Il principe (The Prince):*

> It must be understood that a prince [a ruler] . . . cannot observe all those

Queen Elizabeth I of England promoted scholarship and the arts while still expanding her nation's sphere of influence through exploration and conquest.

Machiavelli's *The Prince*

In the following excerpt from Niccolò Machiavelli's The Prince, *the Italian political writer discusses whether it is better for a ruler to be merciful and loved or cruel and feared.*

"Every prince must desire to be considered merciful and not cruel. He must, however, take care not to misuse this mercifulness. Cesare Borgia was considered cruel, but his cruelty brought order. . . . If this be considered well, it will be seen that he was really . . . merciful. . . . A prince, therefore, must not mind incurring [earning] the charge of cruelty for the purpose of keeping his people united and faithful; for . . . he will be more merciful than those who, from excess of tenderness, allow disorders to arise, from which spring bloodshed and rapine; for these as a rule injure the whole community, while the executions carried out by the prince injure only individuals. . . .

The question [arises] whether it is better to be loved more than feared, or feared more than loved. . . . It is much safer to be feared than loved, if one of the two has to be wanting. For it may be said of men in general that they are ungrateful, . . . anxious to avoid danger, and covetous of gain [greedy]. . . . And the prince who has relied entirely on their words [of loyalty], without making other preparations, is ruined. . . . Men have less scruple [are less hesitant] in offending one who makes himself loved than one who makes himself feared; for love is held by a chain of obligation which, men being selfish, is broken whenever it serves their purpose; but fear is maintained by a dread of punishment that never fails."

things which are considered good in men, being often obliged in order to maintain the state, to act against faith [to break promises], against charity, against humanity, and against religion. . . . He must . . . adapt according to the wind, and as . . . fortune dictate, and . . . do evil if constrained [necessary].[27]

The Spider King of France

The Machiavellian nature of Renaissance rulers is no better illustrated than in the character and actions of the French king Louis XI, who ruled from 1461 to 1483. Known as "the universal spider" because he was constantly spinning webs of intrigue,

Louis turned a medieval kingdom of semi-independent states into the beginning of the French nation.

Born in 1423, Louis started his scheming early. Impatient to become king, he began conspiring at seventeen against his father, Charles VII. His efforts left him in exile during Charles's last five years of life. During that exile, Louis kept tabs on his father through a network of spies, a practice that led to rumors that he had had Charles poisoned. Whatever the truth of these rumors, Charles VII died in 1461, and Louis became the Spider King of France.

The Spider King and the Great Nobles

The new king was little concerned with appearance or ceremony, openly ridiculing tradition and formality. He was stingy, wore cheap, gray clothes and battered felt hats, and ate the same plain food as the French peasants. His castles were dreary and dark, their furniture meager and shabby.

What concerned Louis XI was taming the aristocracy of France, and so upon his taking the throne, he eliminated some of the ancient rights enjoyed by the most powerful aristocrats, the great lords who as rulers of various regions of France were Louis's political rivals. Among other restrictions, he denied these local lords the right to mint their own money, make their own laws, and administer their own courts of justice. He also outlawed the private wars that they fought among themselves. All of these practices were barriers to a united nation.

The great French nobles took poorly to Louis's commands, and many revolt-ed. However, Louis eventually triumphed through a combination of war, diplomacy, and terror. The Spider King defeated some lords in battle, brought others around with promises of expansion of their lands, and silenced others by charging them with treason and then either beheading or imprisoning them.

The Tudors of England

Across the English Channel, the rulers of England were also busy shaping a national monarchy. Beginning with Henry VII in 1485, the English royal family, the

King Louis XI of France stripped the aristocracy of much of its power and worked to create a more unified France.

Renaissance monarchs often tried to strengthen their authority at the expense of the aristocracy. (Left) The Tudors of England created the court know as the Star Chamber to fine or imprison troublesome nobles. (Below) King Ferdinand and Queen Isabella, pictured here with Christopher Columbus, built a monarchy that bypassed the aristocrats and sought loyalty from the commoners.

Tudors, started curbing their own nobility. Particularly troublesome aristocrats were executed, their titles then awarded to newly created nobles, who tended to be grateful to the royal family for their rank and thus loyal to the English monarch.

Somewhat milder but no less effective in dealing with the English aristocracy were the proceedings of the Star Chamber, a court named for the stars painted on its chamber's ceiling. The Star Chamber targeted those nobles who were the most reluctant to submit to the English Crown. This court lacked the authority to sentence the convicted to death, but it could fine them heavily, as well as imprison, brand, and even mutilate them.

Forging the Monarchy of Spain

As France and England moved toward nationhood, a national monarchy was also rising in Spain. In some ways, the Spanish rulers had an advantage over their fellow monarchs, for they were working with a country that had only just come into existence. Spain was formed in 1479 when two of the three kingdoms occupying the Spanish peninsula finally became one under the joint rule of King Ferdinand of Aragon (1452–1516) and Queen

Isabella of Castile (1451–1504). (The third kingdom, Portugal, remained independent.) Together, the king and queen built a new government favoring the monarch, undermining local aristocracies, and supporting militias composed of commoners loyal to the king and queen.

Ferdinand and Isabella did their work well, leaving to their successors the foundation for a strong central Spanish government. As Breisach notes:

> Under the leadership of Isabella and Ferdinand, Spain became the monarchy in which the most consistent and rapid centralization of power in royal hands took place. Royal power began to prevail over the . . . traditional rights of the nobles. . . . Nobles were either attracted to some form of royal service or rigidly kept under control. . . . The alliances of cities . . . with their militia were pressed into royal service. . . . The towns found their economies flourishing.[28]

German and Italian Political Organizations

Not all European regions became national monarchies. Germany and Italy, which had not come under the tight rule of a monarch during the Middle Ages, remained fragmented. Germany was technically part of the Holy Roman Empire, but in reality, it was divided into a number of independent states, each run by its own local lord. During the later Renaissance, these states were also split along religious grounds, those in the north being Protestant and in the south, Catholic. These two factors, continuing local rule and religious differ-

ences, prevented the so-called emperor from creating a strong central government in Germany.

Italy had no central government of any kind. Political power was held by independent city-states such as Milan, Florence, Venice, and Rome, and by Spain, which controlled northern and southern sections of the Italian peninsula. From time to time, France also tried to gain a political foothold in northern Italy.

The New Military

The ambitions of Renaissance monarchs often brought them into conflict with other European rulers. Power struggles between states were a hallmark of the age. These struggles frequently erupted into war and led to the creation of the modern army, which was always on duty and always prepared to fight; its ranks were filled with full-time paid, professional soldiers (the word *soldier* comes from the Latin *solidus,* meaning "a piece of money"). The first of these standing armies was established in France in 1439, and, within a century, a few seafaring countries, such as Spain, had built navies.

The Renaissance army, like its modern counterpart, was divided into ranks of officers and common soldiers. Officers were normally members of the aristocracy, while soldiers belonged to the peasant class. Just as in today's armies, officers drilled their soldiers, teaching them how to parade, dress ranks, and keep discipline.

During this period, no army supplied its members with uniforms. Individual units, however, often dressed alike. Since fighting was often hand-to-hand, soldiers were armed with swords and long pikes. Some units were issued primitive guns, although these were difficult to use because

Lorenzo de' Medici's Advice to the Pope

The complexity of Italian politics is revealed in the following 1489 letter, reprinted from Lorenzo de' Medici: Selected Poems and Prose. *Lorenzo, through his ambassador to Rome, is advising Pope Innocent VIII on how to handle a crisis in Naples. The pope had thrown his support behind a rebellion against King Ferrante, whose claim to the throne of Naples the pope rejected.*

"His Holiness should decide on following one of three paths: enforce his will by war against the King, or come to some agreement, or . . . temporize [compromise] . . . and wait for a better occasion. The first [is not] possible . . . without putting a new ruler over the Kingdom of Naples. For this, . . . either Venice or Milan must be a party to the enterprise . . . , supposing always that Venice adheres [agrees] to the plan and would prevent Milan from helping the King. . . . From what . . . I understand there is no reason that His Holiness should at the present time have this plan or hope, for either Spain or France must be made to intervene to achieve this purpose. Spain does not appear to me strong enough, particularly, as regards money. What reliance is to be placed on France, seeing the French nature [a weak, unintelligent king]. . . . Supposing she changed her nature, I should agree . . . that it would be the best solution, for there would be less danger in augmenting [increasing] the power of the house of Lorraine [French claimant to the Naples's throne] than of Spain, for . . . the King of Naples [Ferrante] is far more close to Spain than the Duke of Lorraine is to France."

early models were big and clumsy and not very accurate.

Ambassadors and Foreign Affairs

The same Renaissance power struggles that gave birth to the modern army also created the modern diplomat. As Ernst Breisach writes,

> [The] continuous maneuvering for power became an important stimulus for the development of diplomacy. Governments simply needed channels of communication, facilities for information gathering, and opportunities to make their influence felt abroad.[29]

The chief means to these diplomatic ends was for a government to have ambassadors living in other countries. This practice, begun in the Renaissance, was the start of today's system of permanently staffed embassies and consulates that most modern governments maintain around the world. As do present-day diplomats, resident Renaissance ambassadors acted as their government's agent or representative, looking after their country's interests abroad. They also sent home regular reports detailing political and social trends in the host countries, as well as describing the character and personalities of local officials and rulers. (The importance of these reports is reflected in how often they were intercepted and stolen by agents of other governments. Such theft eventually required that ambassadorial reports be written in code.)

In addition to resident ambassadors, the governments of Renaissance Europe needed diplomats to attend peace talks and draw up treaties. Each state also came to need a specialized governmental department whose job it was to monitor foreign affairs. Other aspects of government also came increasingly under the management of a professional bureaucracy.

As Renaissance diplomacy evolved, European states worked out rules governing the relations among themselves. Out of these rules grew modern international law. For instance, by the end of the Renaissance, ambassadors and their staffs had achieved some of the privileges common to resident diplomats today. Each was immune to the laws and taxes of the host country, and the ambassador's living quarters were considered to be a part of his native land.

Henry the Navigator and the Way to India

In the fifteenth century, the competition between Renaissance states expanded beyond Europe as sea routes were opened to Asia and the Americas. During this period, known as the Age of Exploration, Renaissance explorers laid the foundations for the European empires that dominated the world for the next several centuries.

The Age of Exploration began in 1421 when Portugal's Prince Henry the Navigator (1394–1460) began sending ships south in search of a way around Africa to Asia. Despite being called the Navigator, Henry himself did not go exploring but instead arranged the financing for voyages of exploration. He also established a school for navigation and mapmaking at Sagres on Cape St. Vincent, the rocky, southernmost tip of Portugal.

Diplomatic Mission

In 1577, the English queen Elizabeth I sent diplomat Edmund Hogan to the Sultan of Morocco to work out a trade agreement between the two countries, both of whom were rivals of Spain. The following account by Hogan is found in Renaissance Letters.

"I arrived off the coast of Barbary [Morocco], at a port . . . called Safia. . . . At the end of five days, the King [sultan] being informed of my arrival sent . . . captains with soldiers and English merchants to me to safeconduct me up to his Court. . . . So to his palace I was brought and to the presence of the King sitting in his chair of state, and his counselors standing about him. I dutifully delivered Your Majesty's letters and declared my message in Spanish, which . . . he well understood. . . . And after, the King gave great thanks to Your Majesty declared that he with his country and all things therein should be at Your Majesty's commandment [command], regarding his honor and law. I answered that Your Majesty reserved [said] the same, as by Your Highness' letters he should perceive. . . . The same night . . . [he] held late conference with me, declaring that the King of Spain had [asked] . . . that he might send an ambassador hither with request that His Honor . . . not give audience to any that might come from Your Majesty, which . . . he had granted, but (said the King) when he [the Spanish ambassador] comes . . . I [will] more . . . of you, coming from the Queen's Majesty of England. . . . I find him [the sultan] agreeable to do good to your merchants more than any other nation; and not to urge any demands of Your Majesty that may tend to your dishonor."

Even after Henry's death, Portuguese ships continued their explorations, traveling ever farther south along the African coast and making detailed maps as they went. Finally, in 1488, Bartolomeu Dias (ca. 1450–1500) rounded the Cape of Good Hope. Ten years later, following Dias's lead, a Portuguese expedition commanded by Vasco da Gama (ca. 1460–1524) reached India.

A New World

In the late fifteenth century, Portugal's new neighbor, Spain, also wanted to find a sea route to Asia, but, blocked by the Portuguese from the south, Spain looked west. In 1492, the Italian Christopher Columbus (1451–1506), sailing for King Ferdinand and Queen Isabella, made

In 1492 Christopher Columbus thought he had sailed to Asia, though he had actually landed in the New World.

landfall on islands in the Americas. The explorer mistakenly thought these islands were part of Asia.

Columbus's error was not discovered until a decade later. In 1501–1502, another Italian, Amerigo Vespucci (1454–1512), working for Portugal, charted the coast of Brazil. Vespucci became convinced that the westward land was not Asia but another continent entirely, which he dubbed the New World.

In 1507, the humanist and geographer Martin Waldseemüller (ca. 1470–ca. 1518) drew the first map showing the New World as a continent. To honor Amerigo Vespucci, the mapmaker called the New World America.

Sailing Round the World

Evidence piled up in favor of Vespucci's claim. In 1513, for instance, the Spanish explorer Vasco Núñez de Balboa (ca. 1475–1519) crossed the Isthmus of Panama and sighted the Pacific Ocean. Many geographers in Europe immediately suspected that this ocean lay between the New World and Asia.

Nine years later, in 1522, final proof came when a Spanish expedition sailed into port after circumnavigating, that is, circling, the earth. Commanded by former Portuguese subject Ferdinand Magellan (ca. 1480–1521), the expedition had been beset with peril and hardship for most of its three-year-long voyage. The Italian historian Antonio Pigafetta (ca. 1491–ca. 1526), who accompanied Magellan, later wrote:

> [We] entered into the Pacific sea, where we remained [without sighting land for] three months and twenty days . . . , and we only ate old biscuits reduced to powder and full of grubs, and . . . we drank water that was yellow and stinking. We also ate . . . the sawdust of wood, and rats. . . . Many suffered, . . . [and] nineteen died.[30]

Later, Magellan himself was killed in the Philippines; of the five ships that set out, only one made it back to Spain. This first circumnavigation of the world, however, established once and for all that the New World was a continent separated by sea from Asia.

Spices and Slaves

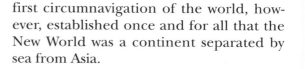

Both Portugal and Spain became wealthy and powerful by exploiting the accomplishments of their explorers. Portugal followed da Gama's voyage with trading missions and was soon importing spices and other luxury goods from India. In 1503, Portuguese traders reached Indonesia, the source of desired spices such as cloves, nutmeg, and pepper, and they

Explorer Ferdinand Magellan (left) commanded the first expedition to circumnavigate the globe. Looking for a navigable waterway through the New World, Magellan eventually rounded the southern tip of South America and reached the Pacific by passing through the straits (right) that bear his name.

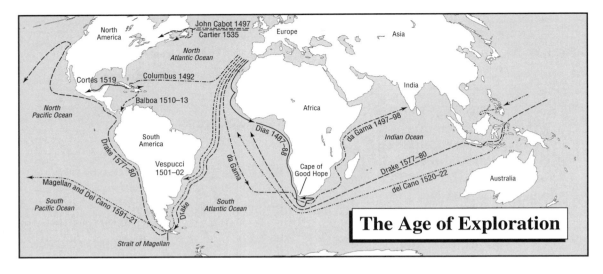

The Age of Exploration

began sending back huge shipments of these valuable seasonings.

But even before Dias rounded the Cape of Good Hope, Portuguese sailors had found a money-making business—slavery. In 1441, the first African slaves arrived in Europe, beginning the centuries-long African slave trade that resulted in the enslavement of millions of blacks. In the early sixteenth century, the Portuguese began selling African slaves to Spanish settlers in the New World. The Spanish enslaved native Americans, but between disease and mistreatment, whole populations of Indians died within the first few decades of European contact, leaving a labor shortage.

Gold and Silver

The Spanish in the New World had found another type of treasure—gold and silver. Much of this gold and silver was in the possession of the two great native American civilizations: the Aztecs of Mexico and the Incas of Peru. This possession led to the conquest of the former in 1521, by Hernando Cortés (1485–1547), and the latter in 1533, by Francisco Pizarro (ca. 1471–1541).

Both cultures had created excellent golden and silver artwork and jewelry. How-

Desiring the riches of the Aztecs, Spanish conquistador Hernando Cortés destroyed the native civilization and sent its wealth back to Spain.

ever, much of it, weighing in the tons, was melted down by the conquerors and shipped back to Spain. When the artifacts ran out, the Spanish used Indian and African slaves to mine for both gold and silver; the silver mines of Peru became a major source of wealth for Spain.

Christian Missionaries

Amassing wealth was not the only important goal of the Portuguese and the Spanish. Spreading Christianity, specifically Catholicism, was another. In a letter to the king of Spain, Cortés wrote that "I instructed them [the Aztecs] . . . to lead them from idolatry and bring them to the knowledge of Our Lord [Christ]."[31] To mark their religious missions, the sails of many Portuguese and Spanish ships had large red crosses painted on them.

Generally, the preaching of Christianity was left to missionaries, many of whom were Jesuits, members of the Society of Jesus. The Jesuits established outposts or missions in most of the non-Christian regions touched by the Spanish and Portuguese. Later, Protestant missionaries would also seek converts all over the world.

Although missionaries converted hundreds of thousands, they had little impact in Asia. India, China, and Japan, as well as other parts of Asia, held firmly unto their own beliefs. In the Americas, where conversion went hand in hand with conquest,

Trade in African slaves was profitable for countries such as Portugal. Slaves were first shipped to Europe in the fifteenth century; by the sixteenth century they were being traded in the New World.

Trade War

During the Age of Exploration, European states often fought to protect trading rights. These battles could be bloody and savage, as illustrated by the following account of a Fugger agent (reprinted in Renaissance Letters*) of a 1589 war between the Portuguese and the Ottoman Turks over Mombassa, an island off the coast of present-day Kenya. This island was an important way station for voyages to India.*

"When . . . [the Portuguese] arrived . . . , they noticed that four Turkish galleys had landed on the coast . . . near a place called Mombassa. On this island the Turks had built a fortress for their protection. . . . Near on three hundred thousand natives [on the mainland] banded together in order to proceed to the island at low tide. . . . For this reason the Turks had removed the cannon from the galleys for their protection, not apprehending [expecting] any danger from the open sea. But the Portuguese . . . intervened, captured the Turkish galleys without resistance, and thereupon landed. When the Turks saw this they sought to take refuge on the mainland, but they were cruelly handled . . . by the wild natives. . . .

The Portuguese general ordered the King of Mombassa, who owes allegiance to the King of Portugal, to be decapitated [beheaded], because he had granted the Turks asylum in his territory. . . . Then the Portuguese left the field clear to the Simbas [mainland natives], who killed . . . the people . . . , so that within five days not a living creature was left there on the island."

---

the missionaries were able to force native Americans to abandon their old religions for Christianity.

Northwest Passage

Other Atlantic-facing countries—France, England, and the Netherlands—were also interested in opening overseas trade routes. In 1497, the English sent an Italian, Giovanni Caboto (1450–1498), better known as John Cabot, to find a northwest route to Asia. Cabot failed but did discover Newfoundland and Nova Scotia. Further English voyages, equally unsuccessful in finding a northwest passage, charted what would be the eastern coast of the United States, the site of future English colonies.

In 1534, the French explorer Jacques Cartier (1491–1557) thought he had found the northwest passage, but it later turned out to be the Gulf of St. Lawrence, an outlet for the St. Lawrence River. However, Cartier's discovery led to the French claiming Canada, which they eventually settled in the seventeenth century.

Trade and Sea Dogs

The failure to find a northwest passage did not keep French, Dutch, and English ships from overseas trading; they often bought and sold Asian goods at Portuguese outposts in Africa. Trade with the Spanish in the New World was more difficult because it was illegal for Spanish settlers to buy from or sell to foreign ships. All such trade was supposed to be done in Spain so that the Spanish government could exercise tight control, thus protecting the Crown's share of the profits.

Some illegal trade with Spanish settlements was possible but not enough to satisfy English sailors, who took to attacking and looting Spanish ships and colonies. These English raiders, known as "sea dogs," were commanded by such captains as Sir John Hawkins (1532–1595) and Sir Francis Drake (ca. 1540–1596), who made their

backers wealthy with plundered Spanish gold and silver. Among the sponsors of the sea dogs was the English queen, Elizabeth I. In 1577, Drake went so far as to sail into the Pacific to find rich prizes. This venture found him repeating the Magellan expedition's around-the-world voyage in order to get home. He arrived back in England in 1580, where in honor of his deed, he was knighted by Elizabeth.

The Spanish Armada

Tensions ran high between England and Spain over the raids of Drake and others. To the English, the sea dogs were heroes; to the Spanish, they were pirates. Eventually, the raids, along with other issues, in particular, religion since England was Protestant and Spain was Catholic, led to war.

The Spanish king, Philip II, decided to invade England, so he assembled a fleet of some 130 warships. Known as the Invincible or Spanish Armada, Philip's fleet and the smaller English navy fought

After being crippled by the highly maneuverable English navy, the remnants of the 130 warships of the Spanish Armada limped homeward. During the retreat, fierce storms claimed ships and their crews.

a series of battles in the English Channel during the first week of August 1588. These engagements went badly for the Spanish, whose ships were outmaneuvered by the English ones. Finally, defeated and blocked from returning south to Spain, the badly mauled armada sailed north around Britain, where it ran headlong into a series of storms that shipwrecked or sank many of the survivors. Only about half the armada returned to Spain; the English did not lose a single ship.

Although the defeat of the armada was a blow to Spain, it was far from a mortal one, as the country still had its colonial empire and all the wealth contained therein. Still, the destruction of the armada meant that England was safe from Spanish invasion. Additionally, to Protestant Europe, the English victory over the greatest Catholic power in the world was greeted as a sign from God, vindicating the break with the Catholic Church.

The Benefits of Exploration

Although the Age of Exploration proved disastrous for the cultures of the New World and for the millions of Africans who were enslaved, it was immensely good for Europe. Its economic effect was slight at first, but the increasing availability of spices and other trade items from Asia allowed people other than the rich to enjoy these luxuries. From the New World came important new foods, potatoes, tomatoes, and corn, and other cash crops such as tobacco.

Geography became more exact as reports from explorers and traders reached Europe. Also becoming more exact and accurate were maps, particularly through the work of Gerhard Kremer (1512–1594), better known as Gerardus Mercator. In 1569, Mercator developed a way to represent the three-dimensional curve of the earth's surface in two dimensions on a sheet of paper. This process, known as a Mercator projection, is still in use today.

Competition among Renaissance states was not confined to European battlefields or to the overseas colonies and trading posts, for the national monarchs also competed with one another to see who could attract the most accomplished artists and thinkers of the period. Indeed, Renaissance courts and royal money, some of it coming from Asian and New World trade, were the major supports of the arts in both Italy and the rest of Europe.

4 Painting and Sculpture

The Renaissance was one of the great ages of art. It was an era of artistic experimentation and discovery, led by Leonardo da Vinci, Michelangelo, Raphael, and many other famous painters and sculptors. These artists left a rich legacy of work, which perhaps more than any other accomplishment represents the Renaissance in today's world.

The Changing Arts

If any one aspect of Renaissance culture differed markedly from the Middle Ages, it was art. During the Middle Ages, the arts had reflected that period's deep interest in religion. Paintings, for instance, were either portraits of Jesus, Mary, and the saints or illustrations of scenes from the Bible.

In the Renaissance, however, art became less religious in nature. Much of it dealt with more worldly subjects, portraits of living people, landscapes, and scenes of everyday life. Not that religious subjects disappeared entirely; indeed, some of the greatest religious art dates from the Renaissance, such as Leonardo's 1497 painting the *Last Supper* and Michelangelo's 1504 sculpture *David*.

Yet, there was a more secular tone to Renaissance art than to medieval art. This artistic shift came in part because the patrons of artists were often nobles and business and civil leaders rather than, as in the Middle Ages, the church. These secular

Raphael's School of Athens *reflects the artistic shift toward secular subjects during the Renaissance.*

In keeping with Renaissance society's new interest in mythological figures, Botticelli's Birth of Venus *depicts the creation of the Roman goddess of love.*

patrons were generally interested in having themselves or their families immortalized in paint or stone.

Additionally, the concerns of Renaissance art were influenced by humanism, with its interest in antiquity and Greek and Roman myths. Many Renaissance paintings and sculptures were of classical subjects, such as Botticelli's *Birth of Venus* (ca. 1480).

The Premier Arts

A second difference between Renaissance and medieval art was the supreme importance of architecture during the Middle Ages. To the medieval world, architecture was the most sublime of arts because architects were responsible for the design and building of the great cathedrals and churches of the period. At this time, both painting and sculpture were used almost exclusively to decorate these church buildings.

In the Renaissance, however, although architecture remained important, painting and sculpture were the chief arts. Again, this change in emphasis had a great deal to do with the rise of the private patron, few of whom, like the Catholic Church, could afford to finance a building but any one of whom could pay for a painting or a statue.

Painters and sculptors benefited socially from the attention patrons paid their arts. During the Middle Ages and into the early Renaissance, artists were considered tradespeople, not unlike carpenters and masons. As Breisach writes:

> Other changes raised the fine arts to a social and cultural position commanding greater prominence [importance]. . . . Patrons began to use art for enhancing [increasing] their social prestige and status. . . . As they used works of art for their conspicuous possession, artists benefited from it by enhancement of their own status. Artistic gifts found a new appreciation and artists gradually occupied a position apart and higher than other craftsmen. Artistic activity came to be regarded as one worthy of serious consideration.[32]

A Realistic Art

A third difference between medieval and Renaissance art was the latter's emphasis on realism. Renaissance artists tried to represent the human figure as realistically and naturally as possible. To achieve this realism, both painters and sculptors studied anatomy and the world around them. They worked hard to portray their painted or sculpted subjects in authentic detail, for as the Italian Leon Battista Alberti instructed in his 1435 *Della pittura (On Painting):*

> It will help, when painting living creatures, first to sketch in the bones, for . . . they always occupy a certain determined position. Then add the sinews and muscles, and finally clothe the bones and muscles with flesh and skin. . . . As Nature clearly and openly reveals all these proportions, so the zealous

[earnest] painter will find great profit from investigating them in Nature.[33]

Because of its close association with the observation of the natural world, this Renaissance realism came to be known as naturalism.

One of the pioneers of Renaissance naturalism was the painter Giotto di Bondone (ca. 1267–1337), who was a native of Florence and a tireless experimenter in technique. Giotto's innovations included adding emotions such as grief, joy, and boredom to the faces of the people in his paintings. He also dressed his people in the everyday clothing he saw about him.

Among sculptors, Donato de Betto di Bardi (ca. 1386–1466), better known by his nickname Donatello, was instrumental in promoting naturalism. Living most of his life in Florence under the patronage of Cosimo de' Medici, Donatello was one of the first Renaissance artists to work in bronze rather than stone. But no matter

Giotto's Lamentation *depicts grief on the faces of its subjects. This expression of human emotion was new to Renaissance art.*

what the material used, he labored to give his sculptures realistic details in order to capture the human personality of his subjects. The realism of Donatello's work led the sixteenth-century art historian Giorgio Vasari to exclaim in his 1550 *Vite de' più ec-* *celenti architetti, pittori ed scultori italiani* (*Lives of the Most Emminent Italian Architects, Painters, and Sculptors*) that the sculptor "brought his figures to actual motion. . . . There is a life-size David . . . so natural . . . that it is almost impossible . . . to believe that it was not molded on the living form."[34]

Donatello's bronze figure David *promotes the expression of naturalism through its realistic details.*

Artistic Perspective

The first of the great naturalistic painters after Giotto was the Italian painter Tommaso di Giovanni di Simone Guidi (1401–1428), better known as Masaccio or Sloppy Tom because of his untidy appearance. Masaccio's paintings in Pisa and Florence during the late 1420s served as the models for much of the later Renaissance art.

To the realistic detail found in Giotto's work, Masaccio added a three-dimensional quality. A Masaccio painting looks like it has depth, with objects and people in the foreground appearing closer and more detailed than those in the background. This three-dimensional effect is known as perspective, and as Leonardo da Vinci would later explain it, "there is no object so large but that at great distance . . . it does not appear smaller than a smaller object near. Among objects of equal size, that which is most remote . . . will look the smallest."[35]

Masaccio learned perspective from a Florentine architect and painter named Filippo Brunelleschi (1377–1446). Brunelleschi in turn became interested in perspective while preparing architectural drawings of buildings. Determined to learn more, the Florentine first read about the subject in a classical book, the *Ten Books on Architecture* by the first-century

The Importance of Painting

In the course of his very technical book On Painting, *written in 1435, Leon Battista Alberti stops to explain why painting is so important.*

"As the effort of learning [how to paint] may perhaps seem to the young too laborious, I think I should explain here how painting is worthy of all our intention and study. Painting possesses a truly divine power in that not only does it make the absent present (as they say of friendship), but it also represents the dead to the living many centuries later, so that they are recognized by spectators with pleasure and deep admiration for the artist. . . . How much painting contributes to the honest pleasures of the mind, and to the beauty of things, may be seen in various ways but especially in the fact that you will find nothing so precious which association with painting does not render [make] far more valuable and highly praised. Ivory, gems, and all other similar precious things are made more valuable by the hand of the painter. . . .

The virtues of painting, therefore, are that its masters see their works admired and feel themselves to be almost like the Creator. Is it not true that painting is the mistress of all the arts or their principal ornament? If I am not mistaken, the architect took from the painter . . . all the . . . fine features of buildings. . . . The sculptor . . . [is] guided by the rule and art of the painter. Indeed, hardly any art, except the very meanest [lowliest], can be found that does not somehow pertain to painting."

B.C. Roman Vitruvius. Brunelleschi then studied geometry, after which he was able to work out the mathematical principles of perspective.

The Use of Oil Paints

Another important breakthrough in Renaissance painting was the development of oil paints, whose use was pioneered by early-fifteenth-century Dutch painters such as Jan and Hubert van Eyck. Prior to oil paints, European artists used the media of fresco or tempera. With fresco, an artist applied paint pigment to the wet plaster of a wall and had to work quickly in order to finish before the plaster dried. Tempera, a mixture of paint pigments, egg yolks, and water, allowed the artist more time, but colors tended to look muddy.

Oil paints, on the other hand, which are mixtures of paint pigments and linseed oil, gave artists a number of advantages over both fresco and tempera. First, oils dried slowly, so an artist could slow his pace. Second, clearer colors with more shades were possible using oils, and the vividness of these colors was easily heightened by coating the painting with varnish. Robert Ergang points out that artists working with oil paints achieved "a workmanship and beauty of color that had been impossible with the use of tempera [and fresco]."[36]

All of this thirteenth- and fourteenth-century experimentation and development laid the foundation in Italy for a great burst of artistic activity known as the High Renaissance. This brief period, which covered the last decades of the fifteenth century and the first few of the sixteenth, included work of many of the greatest Renaissance artists; the two greatest were Leonardo da Vinci and Michelangelo Buonarroti.

Leonardo da Vinci

For a man who listed his profession as painter, Leonardo da Vinci, born in 1452, left behind a mere handful of paintings. But then Leonardo, far more than just a painter, was also an engineer, mathematician, inventor, architect, and writer. Moreover, he was a scientist, whose interest in biology, physics, and chemistry is recorded in 120 notebooks. He was even an accomplished musician, playing a stringed instrument called the lute.

None of these interests kept Leonardo from creating masterpieces. Indeed, the aim of his studies, particularly those in

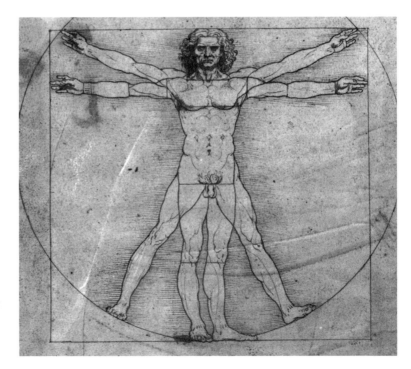

This sketch by Leonardo da Vinci reveals his interest in anatomy, which he studied to improve his paintings.

Leonardo's Advice to a Young Painter

In The Notebooks of Leonardo da Vinci *is found the following advice to young artists.*

"The youth should first learn perspective, then the proportions of objects. Then he may copy from some good master, to accustom [familiarize] himself with fine forms. Then [copy] from nature, to confirm by practice the rules he has learned. . . . Then get the habit of putting his art into practice and work. . . .

It is indispensable to a Painter who would be thoroughly familiar with the limbs in all the position and actions of which they are capable, in the nude, to know the anatomy of the sinews, bones, muscles, and tendons. . . .

The painter . . . must remain solitary. . . . While you are alone you are entirely your own master and if you have one companion you are but half your own, and the less so in proportion to . . . his behavior. And if you have many companions you will fall deeper into the same trouble. . . .

The mind of the painter must resemble a mirror, which always takes the color of the object it reflects and is completely occupied by the images of as many objects as are in front of it. . . . You cannot be a good one [painter] if you are not the universal master of representing by your art every kind of form produced by nature. And this you will not know how to do if you do not see them, and retain them in your mind. Hence as you go through the fields, turn your attention to various objects, . . . collecting a store of divers [varied] facts."

anatomy, was to make his paintings better. He believed firmly that studying the paintings of others alone would produce only minor work. However, a painter who also studied nature would, in his opinion, produce great art.

Leonardo further felt that an artist should not just paint the outer person but,

as he wrote, strive to capture "the intention of . . . [the] soul."[37] Thus, he took painstaking care to reveal through physical detail the character and personality of his subjects, following the advice of Alberti that a painting "will move spectators when the men painted in the picture outwardly demonstrate their own feelings as clearly as

LONDON PUBLIC LIBRARY
20 EAST FIRST STREET
LONDON, OHIO 43140

possible."[38] Thus, in the *Last Supper* (1497), for instance, unlike other Renaissance artists, Leonardo did not physically isolate Judas to reveal the latter's guilt. Instead, Judas is one among the other disciples. His coming betrayal of Christ is revealed through the expression on his face and the posture of his body. The faces and bodies of the other disciples also display their emotions, ranging from horror to sadness to anger to curiosity.

Michelangelo

Somewhat younger than Leonardo was the second of the great High Renaissance artists, Michelangelo Buonarroti, born in 1475. Like Leonardo, Michelangelo's interests were varied, but unlike the former, he put most of his energies into his art, both sculpting and painting.

Michelangelo was a master of perspective, anatomy, and motion, as can be seen in his greatest painted work, the ceiling of the Sistine Chapel at the Vatican in Rome. In four years, from 1508 to 1512, he single-handedly painted close to 350 figures all engaged in major scenes from the Book of Genesis. Michelangelo painted the figures, all anatomically correct, in a range of postures and with faces displaying a variety of emotions.

The same sort of naturalism marks Michelangelo's sculpture. However, he was not necessarily concerned with being literally realistic. In his statue of Moses,

Michelangelo (right), best known for painting the ceiling of the Sistine Chapel in Rome, was another Renaissance artist interested in anatomy and perspective. In his sculpture the Pietá *(left), Mary grieves as she holds the body of Christ.*

for example, the face of the prophet is divided, one half showing compassion, the other, sternness. In the *Pietà,* which shows a grieving Mary holding the body of Christ, the mother's face is younger than the son's because, as Michelangelo explained, "a woman of perfect purity would keep her youth forever." [39]

Northern Europe and Albrecht Dürer

At the same time Leonardo, Michelangelo, and other High Renaissance artists were painting and sculpting in Italy, northern European artists were also doing noteworthy work. In Germany, the painter and engraver Albrecht Dürer (1471–1528), often called the Leonardo of Germany because of the broad range of his interests, advanced the study of perspective and human anatomy. Toward the end of his life, Dürer wrote several studies on these two subjects.

His most important contribution, however, was not in painting but in engraving.

(Above) Michelangelo's The Creation *is just one of many biblical scenes from the Book of Genesis that grace the ceiling of the Sistine Chapel. (Below)* Knight, Death, and Devil *by Germany's Albrecht Dürer illustrates the improvements he made on engraving techniques—improvements that advanced the art of reproducing drawings for books.*

Dürer developed several new techniques that improved the quality of copper engravings and woodcuts. Using Dürer's techniques, printers were able to make reliable reproductions of drawings for books.

Hans Holbein the Younger

Another major northern European artist working in the Italian High Renaissance was Hans Holbein (ca. 1497–1543), also a German. Known as the Younger to distinguish him from his artist father, Holbein spent time in Italy, where he learned composition and perspective, and then in Switzerland, where he met Erasmus, for whom he illustrated *The Praise of Folly*. In 1526 the German artist moved to England, where he spent most of the rest of his life.

In England, he became friends with Sir Thomas More, for whom he painted two portraits, one of the English humanist and another of the entire More family.

The Artist and the Patron

In this 1508 letter, quoted from Renaissance Letters, *the artist Albrecht Dürer defends himself and his work. Dürer's patron, Jacob Heller, felt that the artist was not doing an acceptable job on a painting Heller had commissioned.*

"I am justly surprised . . . that you [Jacob Heller] can accuse me of not holding to my promises to you. From such a slander, each and everyone exempts [excuses] me. . . . I know well what I have written and promised to you, and you know that . . . I refused to promise you to make a good thing, because I cannot. But to this I did pledge myself, that I would make something for you that not many men can. Now I have given such exceeding pains to your picture. . . . I know that when the picture is finished all artists will be well pleased with it. . . . I would not paint another like it for three times the price agreed, for I neglect myself for it, suffer loss, and earn anything but thanks from you.

I am using, let me tell you, quite the finest colors I can get. . . . When the picture is quite finished, I am quite sure that you yourself will say that anything more beautiful you have never seen; but I dare not expect from beginning to end to finish the painting . . . in less than thirteen months. I shall not begin any other work till it is finished, though it will be much to my hurt. . . .

Act in this matter as you will—I will still hold to what I have promised you. . . . If, however, I had not made you a promise I know what I would do."

Hans Holbein the Younger, shown here in a self-portrait, became famous for his portraits of important Renaissance figures, including Henry VIII.

These were the first of many Holbein portraits of Renaissance notables, and it was as a portrait painter that the German became famous. Among Holbein's best known works were paintings of Erasmus in his study and of Henry VIII, for whom Holbein was court painter.

Pieter Brueghel and Everyday Life

Germany was not the only source of northern European artists. From the Low Countries, which had given the Renaissance oil paints, came Pieter Brueghel (ca. 1525–1569). Brueghel was one of the first Renaissance artists to paint scenes from everyday life. Later northern European painters, in-

cluding Brueghel's sons, also became interested in the subject, one that held little interest for Italian artists. Describing these northern artists, Ergang writes:

> Many of [the northern artists] depicted scenes from everyday life. . . . What the painter portrayed was the commonplace, the natural, or something close to nature. . . . The subjects, whether a beggar, children at play, or an old woman threading a needle, were portrayed with the zest of a . . . Michelangelo, . . . thereby contributing much to the ennoblement of mundane life.[40]

Brueghel himself was very interested in peasant life and visited villages, observing and sketching, as well as occasionally joining in village activities. Later, he turned his sketches into paintings of peasant weddings, festivals, and dances. He also did a number of landscapes, detailing the cycle of farm life during the year from plowing to planting to harvesting.

Music

In addition to the visual arts, experimentation was common in the other Renaissance arts. For instance, new, more complex forms of music emerged in France and the Low Countries at the very beginning of the Renaissance. These compositions generally had two or more melodies played simultaneously and woven into a harmonic whole. The interweaving of melodies is known as counterpoint. To play this music, new instruments were invented, among them the violin and the harpsichord.

As did visual artists, musicians found patrons among the powerful and wealthy.

Also as with painting and sculpture, music became more secular, although religious work was still very important, much of it being played during church services in the forms of hymns and Masses. However, even the religious compositions had secular elements as many of them were based on popular folk tunes.

One of the most famous composers of the Renaissance was the Italian Giovanni Pierluigi da Palestrina (ca. 1525–1594), who wrote over five hundred pieces, most of them church music. Known as "The Prince of Music," Palestrina was much admired and imitated, his work becoming models for future music students. Palestrina's compositions, which display a great versatility in their use of musical technique, became increasingly complex and helped pave the way for Baroque music, which dominated the seventeenth century.

An Italian contemporary of Palestrina was Vincenzo Galilei (ca. 1525–1591), father of the famous scientist Galileo Galilei. Although a composer of songs and other music, Galilei was best known for his writings on music theory. In his musical studies, he argued against the Renaissance custom of having a number of singers vocalize simultaneously. Galilei pointed out that this style of singing made it difficult to understand the words. Instead, he championed solo singing, a practice that became more common toward the end of the Renaissance and led eventually in the next century to the development of opera, with its emphasis on one singer vocalizing at a time.

Innovation and invention were also the hallmarks of Renaissance literature. In poetry, prose, and drama, European writers created new forms and produced lasting classics, which continue to influence writers to this day.

5 Poems, Novels, and Plays

The rich artistic legacy of the Renaissance was matched by an equally valuable literary one. It was a period that began with the Italian poet Dante and ended with the English playwright Shakespeare. In between these two authors, many masters worked, experimenting with new forms of literature such as the novel.

The Vernacular

As in art, humanism influenced Renaissance literature through both its ideas and its focus on classical myths and ancient writings, which inspired new forms of poetry and prose on familiar subjects. Yet, one of the most important developments in Renaissance literature did not come from the humanists: This was the expanded use in books and poems of such languages as Italian, French, and English, rather than Latin. Although Latin remained the international language of Europe and was spoken and written by all university-educated people, Renaissance authors increasingly wrote in their native languages. Such local or regional language was known as vernacular.

The feelings of humanists toward the rise of the vernacular were mixed. Some felt that only Latin was appropriate for literature. Others, such as Petrarch, saw the use of the vernacular as a means of passing on classical virtues and knowledge to a far wider audience than was possible with Latin. And, indeed, the rising middle class were more likely to be able to read and write in their own language than in Latin. The scholars Thomas G. Bergin and Jennifer Speake note:

> [Petrarch's] determination that the classical ideal should permeate [soak] every aspect of life led to what has been called the "humanism of the vernacular": the ennobling not only of . . . [the] native tongue, but also of everyday experience under the influence of classical models.[41]

Poets and other writers were generally enthusiastic about the use of the vernacular, feeling that their native languages brought their work alive in a way no ancient, outdated language could. In his 1549 *Défense et illustration de la langue française (The Defense and Illustration of the French Language),* the French poet Joachim du Bellay wrote,

> I cannot wonder at the strange opinion of certain scholars, who think our native language is useless for literature. . . .The time will come . . . when our language . . . will . . . grow enough to equal [that of] the Greeks and Romans

In Defense of the Vernacular

In the 1473 *"Commentary on My Sonnets,"* found in Lorenzo de' Medici: Selected Poems and Prose, *Lorenzo the Magnificent explains why he has chosen to write his poetry in Italian, defending its use as a literary language.*

"If we want to demonstrate the worth of our language [Italian], we need only insist . . . that our language easily express any concept that our minds may have. For this no better argument can be introduced than that from experience.

Our Florentine poets, Dante, Petrarch, and Boccaccio, have in their grave and mellifluous [musical] verses and orations [speeches] shown very clearly and with great facility their ability to express in our language every nuance of meaning. . . .

There is rather a deficiency of men to exploit the language than a deficiency of language available to men and their subject matter. The sweetness and harmony of this tongue, to those who have become accustomed to it . . . , are truly very great and suited to move many people. . . .

Perhaps more works that are subtle, important, and worthy to be read will yet be written in this language, especially since up to now the language has been . . . in its adolescence, for it continually grows more noble and elegant. And it could easily achieve in . . . adulthood still greater perfection. . . . It is enough for the present to draw the conclusion: that our tongue is richly endowed [supplied] with those merits that are intrinsic [natural] to a language, so there is no justification for complaining about it. And for these same reasons no one can reproach [blame] me because I have written in the language in which I was born and nourished."

. . . , producing like them Homers, . . . Virgils, and Ciceros.[42]

Dante and the Vernacular

The first great vernacular writer was the Italian poet Dante Alighieri. Born in Florence in 1265, Dante was active in public affairs until 1302 when his political party fell out of favor and he was exiled from the city. He spent the next twenty years roaming Italy until his death in 1321.

With little else to do, Dante, who had composed some poetry before his exile, turned his full attention to writing. Among his works during this period was

De vulgari eloquentia (On Elegance in the Vernacular Tongue) (ca. 1304), in which he argued that Italian was a suitable language for literature.

In keeping with his position in *De vulgari*, Dante's own *Vita nuova (New Life)* was a collection of poems written in Italian. Finished two years before his banishment from Florence, these poems celebrate Dante's love for Beatrice, whom Dante had first met when they were both children. In the poems, however, Beatrice is not a real person but rather a symbol for an idealized, nonphysical love.

Dante also wrote his masterpiece, the *Divina commedia (Divine Comedy)* in Italian. Begun around 1307, this lengthy poem was the first major western European work to be written in a vernacular. Divided into three sections, the *Commedia* is Dante's imaginary tour of hell, purgatory, and heaven. His guide through the nine circles of hell and along the nine ledges of purgatory is the Roman poet Virgil. However, as a pagan, Virgil cannot enter heaven, and so Dante finishes his tour in the company of Beatrice, who now represents not only love but also spiritual enlightenment.

Petrarch and the Sonnet

Following Dante, the next important experimenter in vernacular writing was Petrarch. Although much of Petrarch's work was in Latin, he wrote a famous sequence of 366 love poems in Italian. Petrarch began

(Left) Dante Alighieri's poetic work the Divine Comedy, *written in Italian, was the first major western European literary work written in a language other than Latin.* (Right) Petrarch's love poems popularized both the Italian sonnet form and sonnet series. The Italian sonnet came to be known as the Petrarchan sonnet.

Dante and the Gluttons

The third circle of hell in Dante's Divine Comedy *is reserved for gluttons, those who eat too much. In the following excerpt, from a prose translation of the poem, Dante and his guide, Virgil, tour the third circle.*

"I am in the third circle of the rain, eternal, accursed, and heavy; its amount and kind never change. Large hailstones, dirty water, and snow pour down through the dark air; the ground that receives them stinks. Cerberus, the fierce and cruel beast, barks doglike with three throats over those submerged there. His eyes are red, his beard greasy and black, his belly large, his paws armed with claws, grasping the spirits [of the gluttons], he flays [strips off the skin] and tears them. The rain makes them howl like dogs; they use one side [of their bodies] to shelter the other; often they turn. . . . When Cerberus the monster saw us, he opened his mouth and showed his teeth. . . . And my leader [Virgil] . . . took some earth and threw handfuls in the ravenous gullet [hungry throat]. As a barking dog, longing for food, grows quiet after he has seized it, since he thinks only of eating, so did those filthy heads of the demon Cerberus who thunders over the shades [the gluttons], making them wish they were deaf. We passed over the spirits subdued by the heavy rain, placing our feet on their nothingness which appears as flesh. They were all lying on the ground. . . . Thus we passed over the filthy mixture of the shades and of the rain, with slow steps."

writing these poems around 1330, finally assembling them, along with some other poems, as the *Canzoniere (Songbook)* (ca. 1349). The whole sonnet sequence deals with Petrarch's love for Laura, a married woman whom Petrarch first met in 1327 and for whom he felt a lifelong, apparently chaste, attachment.

Each of the poems dealing with Laura in the *Canzoniere* is a "sonnet," whose name comes from Italian for "little song." All sonnets have fourteen lines. Some, like Pe-

trarch's, are divided into two sections, the first having eight lines, the second, six. A second sonnet form, developed in England and known as Shakespearean, has three sections of four lines each, followed by a two-line conclusion.

Petrarch did not invent the sonnet, which went back a century before his birth. In Dante's *Vita nuova*, for instance, a number of the poems to Beatrice are sonnets. However, Dante wrote about idealized love, while Petrarch wrote about real longing and desire, which made his sonnets more forceful and appealing. Robert Ergang writes:

> In his sonnets, Petrarch humanized the love theme and brought it down to earth. . . . Petrarch's Laura is a real flesh and blood woman. She is not an ideal figure like [Dante's] Beatrice. . . . It is her body as a human body that excites Petrarch's imagination. . . . Although Petrarch spoke of Laura's inner nature only in vague generalities, he carefully recorded every detail of her physical perfection with the single exception of her nose.[43]

The charm of Petrarch's sonnets made them favorites of many readers, with the form becoming so popular that all Renaissance poets after Petrarch felt compelled to write at least one sonnet cycle, sometimes more. Shakespeare even thought that he would be remembered for his sonnets rather than his plays. Even the Florentine ruler Lorenzo de' Medici "attempted that style that excels all other . . . styles."[44] The sonnet long outlived the Renaissance, remaining a popular verse form for over five hundred years.

Boccaccio and the Storytellers

The third great vernacular writer of Renaissance Italy was Giovanni Boccaccio. Born in 1313, Boccaccio was a contemporary of Petrarch and, like Dante, a Florentine. Sent by his father to Naples to learn business, the fifteen-year-old Boccaccio instead fell in with the humanists of the city and began to write. Between then and his death in 1375, he produced many books as well as works of poetry. Among the books was the first biography of Dante.

Boccaccio's most famous writing is the *Decameron,* which he wrote between 1348 and 1353. This collection of one hundred stories was the first major work of prose fiction in the vernacular, and along with Dante's *Divina commedia* and Petrarch's sonnets, it is one of the great works of Western literature.

The *Decameron* tells of a group of young men and women who spend ten days in the countryside outside Florence while the city is ravaged by plague. On each day, each person tells a story, with the tales ranging from the highly religious

Decameron, *a collection of short tales by Boccaccio (pictured), was the first major prose piece of the Renaissance written in the vernacular tongue. It survives today and is often held up as an example of storytelling at its best.*

Two Sonnets

The following are examples of the two most popular sonnet forms during the Renaissance. The first, known as "Sonnet 1" and taken from Petrarch's Selected Sonnets, Odes and Letters, *has two sections, one of eight lines and one of six. The second, known as "Sonnet 18" and reprinted from* The Complete Works of Shakespeare, *has three sections of four lines each and ends with a two-line conclusion. Both use iambic pentameter, the metered rhythm required for all Renaissance sonnets.*

Sonnet 1

O ye who in these scattered rhymes may hear
The echoes of the sighs that fed my heart
In errant [wandering] youth, for I was then, in part
Another man from what I now appear,
If you have learned by proof how Love can sear,
Then for these varied verses where I chart
Its vain and empty hope and vainer smart [hurt]
Pardon I may beseech [plead], nay, Pity's tear.

For now I see how once my story spread
And I became a wonder to mankind
So in my heart I feel ashamed—alas,
That nought but shame my vanities have bred,
And penance, and the knowledge of clear mind
That earthly joys are dreams that swiftly pass.

Sonnet 18

Shall I compare thee to a summer's day?
Thou art more lovely and more temperate:
Rough winds do shake the darling buds of May,
And summer's lease hath all too short a date [time]:

Sometime too hot the eye of heaven [the sun] shines,
And often in his gold complexion dimm'd;
And every fair from fair sometime declines,
By chance of nature's changing course untrimm'd
    [stripped of decoration];

But thy eternal summer shall not fade
Nor lose possession of that fair thou owest [own];
Nor shall Death brag thou wander'st in his shade,
When in eternal lines [of poetry] to time thou growst
    [live while time lasts]:

So long as men can breathe or eyes can see,
So long lives this [poem] and this [poem] gives life to
    thee.

to the erotic. In general, entertainment was Boccaccio's goal in the *Decameron.* Breisach observes:

> In well-polished prose Boccaccio lays out a panorama of Renaissance society and since he intended to entertain those features prevail which do that best: wayward monks, greedy priests, domineering and tricky women, young lovers, cuckolded husbands [husbands with unfaithful wives], and completely pure heroes and heroines. On occasion a more serious tale pleads a case, such as religious tolerance.[45]

The *Decameron* proved to be immensely popular, even down to today, with readers being delighted by the zest and vigor of the storytelling. Many other writers, both Renaissance and later, would use both the *Decameron* and individual stories as models for poems, novels, short stories, plays, and even movies.

Chaucer and the English Vernacular

One of those writers influenced by Boccaccio was the English poet Geoffrey Chaucer, who was born in 1343. Chaucer was the first great vernacular writer in English, and his long poem about lovers during the Trojan War, *Troilus and Criseyde* (ca. 1383), was based on Boccaccio's piece *Il filostrato* (ca. 1338).

Chaucer's best known work is *The Canterbury Tales,* which was begun around 1387. Although Chaucer apparently never read the *Decameron,* he was familiar with its structure, and the *Tales* is built around a similar gimmick, a group who decide to

The Canterbury Tales *by English poet Geoffrey Chaucer (pictured) is famous for its poetic and often bawdy tales of life during a pilgrimage.*

pass the time telling stories. Chaucer's storytellers are religious pilgrims making a journey to the English cathedral at Canterbury. Like Boccaccio's, Chaucer's stories range from the highly moral to the earthy. Unlike the Italian, however, the English author wrote his stories in verse, not prose. Later English Renaissance authors greatly admired Chaucer; the fifteenth-century poet William Caxton called him the writer who "embellished [dressed up] . . . and made fair our English."[46]

Rabelais and the Novel

In France, the great pioneer in vernacular literature was the French humanist François Rabelais. Born around 1483, Rabelais as a young man became a monk. In

Gargantua's Childhood

The following selection, taken from The Portable Rabelais, *describes in earthy and amusing detail the childhood of the giant Gargantua. The often coarse and broad humor of Rabelais's novel was one of its charms for Renaissance readers.*

"Gargantua, from the age of three to five, was brought up . . . like the little children in the country, namely, in drinking, eating, and sleeping; in eating, sleeping, and drinking; in sleeping, drinking, and eating.

He wallowed in the mud, smudged his nose, dirtied his face, ran his shoes over at the heels, frequently caught flies with his mouth, and liked to chase the butterflies of his father's realm. He . . . wiped his nose on his sleeve, dropped snot in his soup, and paddled around everywhere. He drank out of his slipper [shoe] and ordinarily scratched his belly with a basket. He sharpened his teeth on a top, washed his hands in his porridge, and combed his hair with a goblet [cup]. He would set his butt on the ground between two chairs and cover his head with a wet sack. . . . He struck when the iron was cold, . . . put the cart in front of the oxen, scratched himself where he didn't itch, . . . reached for too much and got too little, . . . beat the bush without getting the birdie, . . . always looked a gift horse in the mouth. . . . His father's pups ate from his plate, and he ate from the plate with them. He bit their ears, they scratched his nose, . . . and they licked his chops."

1524 he found himself in trouble with his superiors for studying Greek, which eventually led to his return to the secular world, where he took up medicine.

Around 1530, Rabelais began to write. He not only experimented with writing in French, but he also tried his hand at a new literary form, the novel. The result was the birth of the French novel in a series of books about the giant Gargantua and his son, Pantagruel. The first of four novels about the pair, *Le Grandes et Inestimables*

Chroniques du grand et énorme géant Gargantua (The Great and Inestimable Chronicles of the Great and Enormous Giant Gargantua), appeared in 1532.

Rabelais's Gargantua and Pantagruel books are satires, whose broad humor is often spiced with playful accounts of the characters' eating, drinking, and lovemaking. Although the books poke fun at all aspects of French and European society, their chief targets are the church and medieval ways of thought, to which many northern European schools still clung. Rabelais's attacks on the old French university, the Sorbonne, led to his having to leave Paris for a time, but in general, the novels were popular and well received.

Cervantes and *Don Quixote*

Another important vernacular Renaissance novelist was the Spanish writer Miguel de Cervantes Saavedra, who was born in 1547. Cervantes's life, until his late fifties, was one of poverty and misfortune. With little formal education, the young Cervantes sought his fortune by joining the Spanish army. During this military service, he was wounded in battle, losing the use of his left hand. Later, on his way home to Spain, he was captured by Ottoman Turks and imprisoned for five years.

After his release and return to Spain, Cervantes began writing plays and stories, hoping to make a living. Although his plays had some success, in general, he barely scraped by. Indeed, at least twice in his life, the struggling author went to jail because he could not pay his debts.

Cervantes's fortune changed in 1605 with the publication of the first part of his novel *Don Quixote*. Tremendously popular then and now, this novel presents the humorous adventures of Don Quixote, an old Spanish aristocrat who thinks that he is a medieval knight. His delusion leads him

(Left) Miguel de Cervantes Saavedra became a popular Renaissance author when he wrote Don Quixote, *a novel that chronicled the adventures of a delusional Spanish aristocrat and his peasant sidekick, Sancho Panza. (Right) In this engraving by Gustave Doré, Cervantes's protagonist, Don Quixote, battles a windmill he believes is a ferocious giant.*

Legal Action over *Don Quixote*

The novel Don Quixote *was so popular and its sale so profitable that many illegal editions were published. In the following 1605 letter, quoted in* Renaissance Letters, *Cervantes authorizes legal action against those responsible for the unauthorized editions.*

"Let all those who see this letter . . . know that I, Miguel de Cervantes Saavedra, . . . having composed a book entitled *The Ingenious Knight Don Quixote de la Mancha,* our lord king has given and granted his . . . license, . . . that I or anyone whom I empower [appoint] . . . may print and sell the work in the Kingdoms of Castile and Portugal for a period of ten years, forbidding . . . that any other individual without my authorization or permission may print or sell it. . . . It has come to my notice that a few persons . . . have printed or intend to print the aforesaid book without my authorization or permission. . . . I am conferring all my full . . . power . . . on Francisco de Robles, royal bookseller, the lawyer Diego de Alfaya, and Francisco de Mar, . . . each singly or as a group . . . , to initiate criminal action in the proper way and form against the person or persons who have, without my permission, printed the aforesaid book in any region of the Kingdoms of Castile or Portugal. Let them seek punishment and sentencing of those persons under the royal law, submitting in my name petitions, . . . demands, citations, protests, . . . documents and proofs. Let them request embargoes, surrenderings, imprisonments, . . . and let them put the accused under oath and submit them to all other judicial . . . inquiry."

into all sorts of trouble, as he battles windmills that he believes are giants and tries to save a peasant girl who he is convinced is a princess.

Accompanying Don Quixote on his travels is another Spanish peasant, Sancho Panza, whose realistic view of life Cervantes contrasts amusingly with the old knight's unworkable idealism. By the end of part two of the novel, published in 1615, the year before Cervantes's death, Don Quixote and Sancho Panza have encountered a large cast of characters and stumbled through many adventures, all of which spotlight the ills of Spanish and Renaissance society.

Lope de Vega, Man of Fifteen Hundred Plays

Working at the same time as Cervantes was another important Spanish vernacular writer, Lope Félix de Vega Carpio, born in

1562. A ladies man and adventurer, Lope de Vega had countless love affairs and sailed with and survived the defeat of the Spanish Armada by the English navy in 1588. In between, he wrote poems, novels, and plays. His poetry ran the range from Petrarchan love sonnets to song lyrics to historical epics. Around 1590, he wrote his first novel, *Arcadia,* which deals with the joys of country life.

But it was as a playwright that Lope was most famous. His contemporaries reported that he wrote around fifteen hundred plays, of which some five hundred survive today. Although Lope favored comedies, he also wrote serious dramas.

Author Lope de Vega found fame as a playwright specializing in comedies based on Spanish history, folk tales, legends, and myths.

He took the plots for his plays from all sorts of sources, including Spanish history, folk tales and legends, ancient myths, and the Bible. His characters are not particularly realistic, although their speech accurately represents their social class.

Around 1607, Lope wrote a humorous poem, "Arte nuevo de hacer comedias" ("The New Art of Making Comedies"), in which he gave his formula for writing successful plays. He noted that a dramatist could rarely go wrong with the *capa y espada (cloak and dagger)* plot, in which upper-class characters engage in intrigue, love affairs, and sword fights.

Christopher Marlowe and the English Stage

At the same time that Lope was swamping the Spanish stage with his productions, playwrights in England were creating many of the major vernacular dramas of the Renaissance. The English theater of the last half of the 1500s, the reign of Queen Elizabeth I, was popular with all social classes. These appreciative Elizabethan audiences were entertained by the works of a large number of dramatists, of whom the two greatest were Christopher Marlowe and William Shakespeare.

Christopher Marlowe, born in 1564, is something of a mystery man. A graduate of Cambridge University, he appears to have been a government spy, even while still in school. He reportedly traveled to other countries on secret missions, the details of which are lost. His death is just as shrouded in mystery as his spying activities. He died young at the age of twenty-nine, supposedly killed in a brawl over a tavern bill. Yet, to this day, rumors circulate that he was assassinated.

No matter the true circumstances of his death, in his short life Marlowe wrote half a dozen of the most popular plays of the Elizabethan period. Some, such as the two parts of *Tamburlaine the Great* (1587) and *The Troublesome Reign and Lamentable Death of Edward the Second* (1594), are grand, sweeping historical plays. Others, like *The Tragical History of Dr. Faustus* (ca. 1589) and *The Famous Tragedy of the Rich Jew of Malta* (ca. 1590), are tragedies, in which personal flaws bring down the lead characters.

A number of factors made Marlowe's plays so popular with the Elizabethans. First, he wrote using vivid and forceful language. Second, he populated the stage with dynamic characters, who develop and change during the course of the play. Third, he researched his plays to make them more realistic. Finally, he added large doses of intrigue, action, and violence.

William Shakespeare, the Great Dramatist

Marlowe was not the only playwright of his day who knew how to use language, to develop characters, and to drive plots with action and violence. Indeed, he had any number of competitors, one of whom, William Shakespeare, would surpass him in both ability and fame.

Shakespeare, born at Stratford-upon-Avon in 1564, arrived in London sometime in the late 1580s. There, he eventually joined one of the city's leading theater companies, Lord Chamberlain's Men, later known as the King's Men. Shakespeare did some acting with the troupe, but his pri-

mary duty was to write plays, which he began doing around 1589 with the three parts of *Henry VI*. He quickly followed with a series of history plays, comedies, and tragedies, which included *Richard III* (ca. 1592), *The Taming of the Shrew* (ca. 1594), and *Romeo and Juliet* (ca. 1595). Beginning in 1600, at the height of both his popularity and his creativity, Shakespeare wrote his four great tragedies, *Hamlet* (ca. 1600), *Othello* (ca. 1605), *King Lear* (ca. 1605), and *Macbeth* (ca. 1606). He died in 1616, and seven years later, his friends published the first collection of his plays, known as the First Folio.

Shakespeare's dramas were even more popular than Marlowe's, and his success made him rich within a decade of his arrival in London. Audiences enjoyed his

The most revered writer in English literature, William Shakespeare wrote poetry and plays that are still appreciated today. The Elizabethan or English sonnet form that he made famous is also referred to as the Shakespearean sonnet.

Shakespeare performs one of his plays for the Elizabethan court. Some of the playwright's most famous works include: Hamlet, King Lear, Romeo and Juliet, *and* Macbeth.

clever and imaginative use of English, his vivid characters, and his elaborate plots, which in the later plays hinge upon the personalities on the stage. And it is these same elements that have made him the most famous writer in English literature. Even today, four hundred years later, his plays are read and seen by more people all over the world than the dramas of any other playwright living or dead. His plays have served as the basis for other plays, operas, and movies. As his fellow Elizabethan dramatist Ben Jonson observed in the First Folio, "he was not of an age, but for all time."[47] Crane Brinton adds, "Shakespeare . . . continues, even outside the English-speaking world, to be a kind of George Washington of letters [literature], above reproach. He is the necessary great writer."[48]

Poets and Essayists

In addition to playwrights, the Elizabethans also produced a number of other accomplished writers. It was an age of poets. Some, such as the explorer and politician Sir Walter Raleigh, merely dabbled in verse. Others, however, took poetry more seriously.

Among the latter was Edmund Spenser, born about 1552. Spenser's major work was *The Faerie Queene,* begun around 1580 and left unfinished upon the poet's death in

1599. This long poem, written in a very difficult rhyme scheme that now bears Spenser's name, is set in a medieval kingdom meant to represent Elizabethan England. Spenser loaded the poem with a host of then-current religious and political issues.

Prose writers also flourished during the Elizabethan period, one of the most accomplished of whom was Sir Francis Bacon, born in 1561. Beginning in 1597, Bacon wrote a series of essays in which he reflected upon such topics as truth, death, atheism, and marriage. However, his most important writing dealt with the newly emerging experimental science of the Renaissance. One of the most important legacies of the period, European science would become, as Nauert points out, "the most exportable Western commodity, . . . [penetrating] anti-Western civilizations that have easily resisted . . . Western religion, Western philosophy, and Western artistic and literary traditions."[49]

6 Science and Medicine

The intellectual energies of the Renaissance went not only into art and literature but also into science and medicine. During the last century of this era, new discoveries, particularly in astronomy, physics, and anatomy, led to increased understanding of the natural world.

The Beginnings of Science

Vital to the growth of scientific investigation was a gradual rejection of astrology and magic, belief in which was common during the Middle Ages. Sir Francis Bacon warned in his 1620 *Novum Organum (New Organ)* that these superstitions were harmful to the pursuit of science: "The corruption of philosophy [science] by . . . superstition . . . is most injurious to it both as a whole and in parts." Later, he added that "there is . . . much difference in philosophy between their [superstitions'] absurdity and real science."[50] In general, the scientists of the day rejected any sort of magic because it was not supported by observation and experimentation, although a few astronomers, such as Tycho Brahe, continued to believe that the stars did affect human destiny.

Equally important to the development of science was humanism, for among the ancient writings that the humanists collected were those that inspired scientific research. As the astronomer Nicolaus Copernicus wrote in 1543, "I took the trouble to reread all the books by [ancient] philosophers which I could get hold of."[51] Impressed after reading the studies of such ancient Greeks as Archimedes and Hero of Alexander, some Renaissance scholars decided to try their own hand at teasing out the secrets of nature.

Numbers and Symbols

Additionally, Renaissance scientists discovered in these ancient works a powerful tool: mathematics. Renaissance philosophers began using mathematics to discover the relationships between observed events, and it was during the Renaissance that math and science became closely linked. Indeed, many of the great scientists of the day, such as Kepler and Galileo, trained first as mathematicians. According to Stephen Toulmin and June Goodfield, "The idea grew that *mathematical axioms* were the true principles of things. In order to explain why things are as they are and behave as they do, . . . [things must] conform to certain mathematical equations."[52]

Among the math discoveries of the Renaissance was the usefulness of negative numbers, those less than zero, first proposed in 1545 by the Italian Girolamo Cardano (1501–1576). In the same year, Cardano published the first important European book on algebra, *Ars Magna (The Great Art),* which contained the solution to cubic equations (solving for x^3) and quartic equations (solving for x^4). Cardano later wrote one of the earliest studies on probability.

Another important mathematical innovation of the period was the decimal. Introduced in 1586 by Simon Stevin (1548–1620), a mathematician of the Low Countries, decimals are a different way of writing fractions, making it easier to add, subtract, multiply, and divide fractional quantities. Their use immensely simplifies complex calculations.

A few years later, in France, François Viète (1540–1603) proposed in his 1591 book *In artem analyticem isagoge (Introduction to the Analytical Arts)* that letters, such as *x, y,* and *z,* be substituted in algebraic formulas for known and unknown quantities, which up till then had often been written out as full words and phrases. Viète's proposal created a flexible mathematical language that made such higher math as calculus possible.

Humanism and Science

The humanists might supply the classical texts to Renaissance scientists and mathematicians, but in general, they rejected research. Most of them firmly believed that everything that could be known was already included in the books of antiquity. They also thought that the old Greek and Roman writers could never be wrong in any of their facts or conclusions. The scholar Anthony Grafton writes:

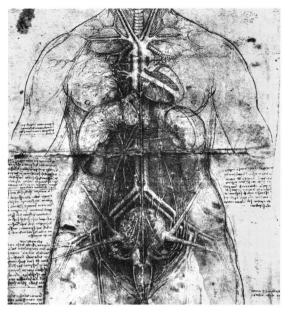

Though relying on the authority of classical texts may have blinded some Renaissance scientists, the era proved to stimulate advances in both abstract sciences and some practical sciences such as anatomy.

> The humanists had failed to see that the world had changed . . . [that] modern technology [was] more powerful than those of the ancients. They had confused . . . the fact that their texts had existed for a long time . . . with the authority that human beings gain as they age—an authority that can only be invested in [granted to] people, who continue to learn as they age, not in books, which are impervious to [cut off from] experience.[53]

Leonardo da Vinci, for instance, genius though he was, could not shake off

Bacon Versus the Ancients

In his 1620 Novum Organum (New Organ), *Sir Francis Bacon argues that Renaissance thinkers need to shake off their reliance on the ancient Greeks and Romans, whose knowledge was inferior to that being collected by Renaissance explorers and scientists.*

"The reverence for antiquity, and the authority of men who have been esteemed [judged] great in philosophy . . . have retarded men from advancing in science, and almost enchanted them. . . .

The opinions which men cherish of antiquity is altogether idle. . . . As we expect a greater knowledge of human affairs . . . from an old man than a youth, on account of his experience, and the variety and number of things that he has seen, heard, and meditated upon, so we have reason to expect much greater things of our own age . . . than from antiquity since the world has grown older. . . .

We must also take into our consideration that many objects in nature . . . have been exposed to our view, and discovered by means of long voyages and travels, in which our times have abounded [swarmed]. It would . . . be dishonorable . . . if . . . the earth, the sea, and stars should be so . . . developed [explored] . . . in our age, and yet the boundaries of the intellectual globe should be confined to the narrow discoveries of the ancients.

With regard to authority, it is the greatest weakness to attribute [give] infinite credit to particular authors. . . . For truth is rightly named the daughter of time, not of authority. It is not wonderful . . . if antiquity . . . [and] authority . . . have so enchained the power of man, that he is unable . . . to become familiar with things themselves."

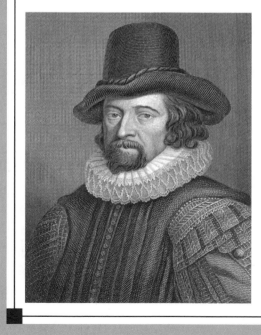

Sir Francis Bacon acknowledged that Renaissance science was progressing from its classical roots.

this acceptance of classical authority while studying the way blood moved through the human heart. The ancient expert on these matters was the second century A.D. Greek physician Galen, who claimed that clearly visible pores let blood flow from one chamber of the heart to another. Such pores do not exist. But when Leonardo could not find them, he decided that he, not Galen, was mistaken.

The Renaissance Theory of Science

However, Leonardo did not always give way to ancient authority. His studies of the geology of the Po River valley convinced him that the entire area was at least two hundred thousand years old, making the earth far older than classical authorities claimed.

Leonardo in his haphazard way, as well as other Renaissance scientists in more determined fashion, showed the importance of observation, particularly when linked to experimentation, for any type of research. Up till this time, most philosophers followed the common practice in ancient Greece and Rome of using logic alone to get at the laws of nature. These logic-produced theories were tested only with more logic rather than by devising an experiment to show whether or not they worked in the real world.

In 1605, Sir Francis Bacon argued in his *Advancement of Learning* that logic must be supported with information gained from experiments in order for any theory to be judged correct. Then, the conclusion drawn from this information must be tested with further experiments. Bacon's scientific method underlies all scientific

research in the present-day world. Nauert points out:

> Bacon . . . saw . . . that the new "natural philosophy" (or "science" as we would call it) would have to be experimental and that scientific conclusions would have to be demonstrated theories. . . . Bacon realized that the logic of science would have to direct the mind in processing from observed phenomena (experimental data) to broad generalizations.[54]

Copernicus and the Moving Earth

Bacon did not invent the scientific method; it had already been in use for

Nicolaus Copernicus derived through mathematics that the earth rotated around the sun. His theory met with disbelief from theologians as well as many humanists.

The Moving Earth

In the two following excerpts, the Protestant clergyman Andrew Osiander and the Polish astronomer Nicolaus Copernicus ask Renaissance philosophers to keep an open mind about the proposal that it is the earth, not the sun, that moves through space. The first selection is Osiander's introduction to Copernicus's On the Revolutions of the Heavenly Spheres, *and the second is Copernicus's preface to the same book.*

"Since the newness of the hypothesis [theory] of this work . . . has already received a great deal of publicity, I have no doubt that certain of the savants [philosophers] have taken grave offense and think it wrong to raise any disturbance among . . . disciplines which have had the right set-up for a long time now. If, however, they are willing to weigh the matter scrupulously, they will find that the author of this work has done nothing which merits blame. For it is the job of the astronomer to use painstaking and skilled observation in gathering together the history of the celestial [astronomical] movements and then . . . to think up . . . hypotheses such that . . . these same movements can be calculated from the principles of geometry. . . . This artist [Copernicus] is . . . outstanding in both of these respects."

"I am sure that talented and learned mathematicians will agree with me, if . . . they are willing to give not superficial but profound thought and effort to what I bring forward in this work in demonstrating these things. . . . If . . . there are certain 'idle talkers' who . . . pronounce judgment, although wholly ignorant of mathematics . . . ; they worry me so little that I shall even scorn their judgments as foolhardy."

some time. Indeed, it lay at the heart of the scientific work of Polish astronomer Nicolaus Copernicus. Born in 1473 and educated at universities in both Poland and Italy, Copernicus forever changed the way Western civilization looks at the universe and in the process launched modern astronomy. At Copernicus's birth, Europeans believed that the earth was stationary, the center of the universe. All other heavenly bodies, including the sun, re-

volved around the earth. This belief had been passed to the Renaissance in the writings of classical astronomers.

However, Copernicus used observation and mathematical analysis to overturn this concept. With instruments he built himself, the astronomer studied the night sky for years, while taking careful notes. Calculations using this collected information showed him that it was the earth, not the sun, that moves. Copernicus realized that the earth both revolves around the sun and rotates about its own axis. The Polish scientist eventually published his findings in the 1543 *De revolutionibus orbium coelestium (On the Revolutions of the Heavenly Spheres)*.

The Reaction to Copernicus

Copernicus's theory, known as Copernicanism, was met with a mixture of disbelief and hostility since it contradicted classical astronomy. Indeed, the Polish astronomer had finished *De revolutionibus* thirteen years before its publication but had initially decided not to publish it because he had feared the reaction of critics. In fact, he almost abandoned the whole project, writing that "the scorn which I had to fear on account of the newness and absurdity of my opinion almost drove me to abandon a work already undertaken."[55]

In addition to contradicting the ancients, Copernicanism aroused hostility for another important reason. His theory was seen as a threat to humanity's place in the cosmos. While the earth was the center of the universe, so were humans and their concerns. But with the earth shifted from that center, so were people, and their cosmic importance, as well as their relationship to the universe, became less certain. Many philosophers, particularly theologians, bitterly resented and resisted this lessening of human importance.

Tycho Brahe's Universe

Not all Renaissance scholars and philosophers rejected Copernicus's ideas. The Danish astronomer Tycho Brahe, born in 1546, sought a compromise between Copernicus's ideas and classical astronomy. Although Brahe refused to believe that the earth was not the center of the universe, he conceded that the other planets did revolve around the sun. However, he proposed that the sun in turn spun around the earth.

Despite his mistaken view of the solar system, Tycho Brahe was an important astronomical pioneer in his own right. He was one of the greatest observational astronomers who ever lived. And he did all his work before the invention of the telescope, observing stars, planets, and other heavenly objects with his naked eye at his observatory Uraniborg, located on an island near Copenhagen.

It was Brahe who first showed that comets moved in space far beyond the moon and were not, as commonly believed, part of the earth's atmosphere. Even more important, the Danish astronomer made painstaking observations of the position of stars and the movements of the planets. These observations allowed him to be the first to pinpoint the exact location of almost eight hundred stars, information important to later astronomers.

Kepler and the Planets

If Tycho Brahe could not wholeheartedly embrace Copernicanism, other astronomers could and did. One was Brahe's colleague, the German Johannes Kepler (1571–1630), who inherited the Dane's papers upon the latter's death in 1601. Kepler used Brahe's careful observations to make important discoveries about the mo-

After the beginning of a tremendous enterprise [Copernicanism] has been made in our time, and furthered by so many learned mathematicians, and after the statement that the earth moves can no longer be regarded as something new, would it not be better to pull the rolling wagon to its destination [acceptance of the theory] with united effort? . . . If I am not mistaken, there are only a few among the distinguished mathematicians of Europe who would dissociate [separate] themselves from us. So great is the power of Truth.[56]

Falling Bodies and the Telescope

And indeed, no more vocal defender of Copernicanism existed during the Renaissance than this Italian astronomer and mathematician, Galileo (1564–1642). Kepler's letter reached Galileo about the time the latter was becoming interested in astronomy. Up to this time, the Italian's energies had gone into a series of experiments with falling objects, first described in his 1591 book *De motu (On Motion).* Galileo showed, among other things, that both light and heavy bodies fall at the same rate. This conclusion brought a storm of criticism from many philosophers because Galileo's conclusion challenged Aristotle, who had claimed just the opposite. Galileo, however, was putting into practice what Sir Francis Bacon would put into words a decade and a half later: "Study . . . things themselves. Be not for ever the property of one man."[57]

Improving on imperfect models of planetary orbits, German astronomer Johannes Kepler demonstrated that the planets traced elliptical paths around the sun.

tion of the planets. In his 1609 book *Astronomia nova (New Astronomy),* the German astronomer was able to show that the orbits of the planets were ellipses, that is, oval-shaped, and not circles as was traditionally believed. Kepler's conclusion provided a simpler and more workable model for the solar system than any previous one. It also paved the way for the English scientist Sir Isaac Newton's theories on gravity in the next century.

Kepler's planetary motion depended upon the planets, including the earth, revolving around the sun. An enthusiastic supporter of Copernicanism, he campaigned tirelessly for this theory. In a 1597 letter to the Italian scientist Galileo Galilei, Kepler urged that the two form a united front to promote Copernicus's theory:

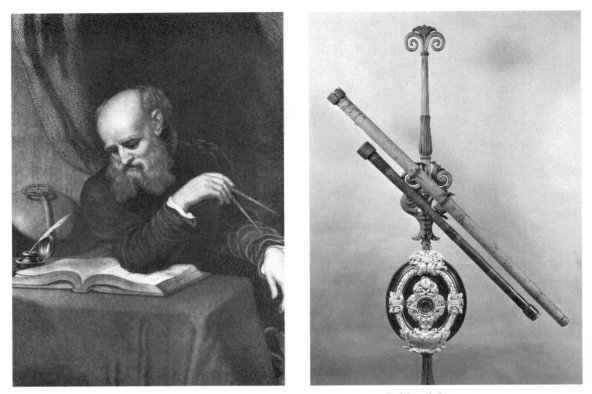

Incorporating a Dutch tool used for sea navigation, Italian astronomer Galileo (left) constructed a telescope (right) for observing the heavens. With this device he viewed the surface of the moon and discovered other satellites orbiting the planet Jupiter.

Studying the heavens, however, was more difficult. The human eye could only see so much, and because of this limitation, little evidence existed to support Copernicanism through the end of the sixteenth century. In 1608, matters quickly changed with the invention of the telescope in the Low Countries. Although credit for the invention generally goes to the spectacle-maker Hans Lippershey, a number of individuals arrived at the idea simultaneously.

Galileo was quick to grasp the telescope's importance to astronomical observation, so he built his own. In late 1609, he turned his new instrument skyward. One of his first discoveries was that the moon's surface was covered with craters, mountains, and valleys. This observation pleased him, for it destroyed another Aristotelian claim that heavenly bodies were perfect, lacking blemishes or defects.

Galileo's second great discovery pleased him even more and gave him ammunition against critics of Copernicanism. In early 1610, he spotted the four largest moons of Jupiter. Copernicus's critics had wanted to know why an earth moving around the sun did not leave the moon behind. Although Galileo still could not explain why the moon kept pace with the earth, he now could point to a known moving planet,

Jupiter, that carried its orbiting satellites with it. Why, he asked, should a moving earth and its moon be any different?

Dialogue and Trial

Galileo continued to argue vigorously for Copernicus's ideas, ignoring advice from friends to keep his opinions to himself be-cause his blunt and often insulting comments were making powerful enemies, particularly among the supporters of Aristotle. In 1632, he published his *Dialogo sopra i due massimi sistemi del mondo (Dialogue on the Two Great World Systems)*, which clearly shows his enthusiasm for Copernicanism and his contempt for Aristotelianism. Aristotelians in the church soon convinced the pope that Galileo's attack on Aristotle, whose writings had long

Galileo on Trial

The following 1633 letter, written by Cardinal Vincenzio da Firenzuola and reprinted in Renaissance Letters, *gives an account of the events leading up to Galileo's renouncing Copernicanism during his heresy trial.*

"Yesterday . . . their Eminences of the Holy Congregation [the Inquisition] took up the case of Galileo. . . . Having approved what had been done thus far, they then considered various difficulties as to the manner of prosecuting the case, and getting it speedily under way. . . . In particular because Galileo denied . . . that which is evident in the book he wrote, it would necessarily follow from his negative attitude that there would be greater rigor in the proceedings [torture]. . . . I proposed a means: that the Holy Congregation grant me power to deal . . . with Galileo to the end of convincing him of his error, and bringing him to the point . . . of confessing it. It appeared at first sight too daring a proposal; there seemed little hope of succeeding by means of reasonable persuasion; but they gave me the power. . . . I went to reason with Galileo yesterday . . . , and after many exchanges between us, I gained my point . . . , for I made him see plainly his error, so that he clearly knew that he was in the wrong, and that his book had gone too far. . . . He agreed to confess it. . . . The Tribunal will maintain its reputation . . . and may use benignity [leniency] with the accused. . . . This done it will be possible to return him to his house for imprisonment."

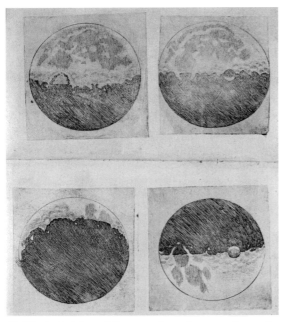
Galileo's sketches of the moon's surface, as observed through his telescope.

rived at through painstaking observation, which in Galileo's case often meant experimentation and careful record keeping. For example, the success of Galileo's falling-body studies depended upon reliable records of times and distances. Galileo used the information from these records to work out the mathematical relationships involved in his experiments. Copernicus, Brahe, and Kepler made similar calculations, and in doing so, they and Galileo helped create modern science.

Medicine and Anatomy

Renaissance advances in other sciences were not as dramatic or as sweeping as those coming from Copernicus, Kepler, and Galileo, although another physical science, geology, fared well during the period. Geology was tied to mining, one of the most profitable of Renaissance industries, and its study was encouraged by mine owners. The 1556 mining handbook, *De re metallica (All About Metals)*, written by the German geologist Georgius Agricola, gives very clear and useful descriptions of different kinds of soils and rocks.

The biological sciences saw only a little real progress during the Renaissance. Biology and botany were confined to half-hearted stabs at creating catalogs of animals and plants. The related field of medicine, however, made some progress during the Renaissance, although in general doctors still held tightly to ideas proposed by Galen. In part, medical progress was spurred on because of the appearance in the fourteenth century of the

since become an important part of church doctrine, was an attack against Catholicism. They emphasized the danger by pointing out that the *Dialogue* was written in Italian, not the usual Latin, and so its potential audience was very large, as was the potential harm to the church.

The pope had publication of the *Dialogue* stopped within six months of its appearance and had Galileo brought to trial for heresy, at the end of which the scientist publicly abandoned Copernican thought. The alternative was torture and death. Despite his forced denial, Galileo never lost faith in the Copernican system, and other Renaissance astronomers would perform observations that would eventually lead to the general acceptance of the moving earth and the fixed sun.

The conclusions reached by Copernicus, Brahe, Kepler, and Galileo were ar-

Black Death, or bubonic plague, and in the fifteenth of syphilis. Neither disease had been known to Galen, and thus, Renaissance doctors were forced to experiment if they wanted to find treatments. They were unsuccessful in halting the devastating plague, but a German physician, Theophrastus Bombast von Hohenheim, known as Paracelsus, discovered in 1530 that drinking mercury compounds was an effective treatment for syphilis.

The greatest advance in the medicine of the period was an increased understanding of human anatomy, due in large part to the work of Andreas Vesalio, better known as Vesalius. Born in 1514 in the Low Countries, Vesalius was the son and grandson of doctors. After studying medicine in Paris, he became interested in human anatomy, hoping to improve on the information passed down by Galen. Unlike the ancient Greek, who had depended

Bad Medicine

Although some advances were made in medicine during the Renaissance, most medical practice was bad, as can be seen in excerpts from two letters quoted in Renaissance Letters. *The first was written by Pietro Aretino in 1537 and the second by Bishop Antonio de Guevara to his personal physician in 1525.*

"As far as I am concerned, I compare medicines to the raging of a torrential stream which carries away whole fields and not merely boulders and the trunks of trees. I insist that these villainous concoctions [mixtures] suck out months and years from your vitals, leaving life itself all withered away. . . .

The presumption [belief] that intoxicates them [doctors] stakes an ounce of health against the full measure of two lives, and our ignorant laws decree that they shall not be punished but praised for their homicides."

"I still have my gout [painful crystalline deposits in joints]. I ordered those herbs and roots and, as per your instructions, I got them out, chewed them, and even drank them, and may God grant salvation to your soul if they . . . [did] anything for my gout. They merely heated up my liver and chilled my stomach. I must confess that you not only failed to diagnose my illness, but even made it worse. The chill in my stomach makes me keep belching. . . . I don't understand why you are punishing my stomach, the chief villain being my ankles. . . . There is nothing in the world which makes me lose my mind . . . than the way doctors treat someone, for we see them eager to cure and enemies of effecting [achieving] cures."

Advances in medical sciences during the Renaissance came primarily from the need to treat victims of the bubonic plague (left) and from the studies of human anatomy conducted by Vesalius (right).

mostly on the dissection of animals, Vesalius used human bodies whenever possible. By keeping an open mind and a sharp eye for detail, the Renaissance anatomist improved on and corrected Galen's work.

In 1543, Vesalius published *De humani corporis fabrica (On the Structure of the Human Body),* in which he described his findings. Accompanying the text were detailed illustrations made from very accurate woodcut diagrams. *De humani* quickly became the standard human anatomy text of its time.

The Gregorian Calendar

One of the burning issues of the Renaissance was calendar reform. The calendar of the time, inherited from the Romans, was based on a year of 365.25 days. During every fourth year, or leap year, an extra day was added to cancel that quarter day.

However, the partial day in each year was not exactly a quarter-day long. Although the difference was small, over two thousand years of use, the calendar was running ten days too fast by the late sixteenth century. Thus, for instance, according to the calendar, the spring equinox, whose date was supposed to be March 21, fell on March 11.

To the Catholic Church, this difference was critical because the date of the spring equinox was used to calculate the celebration of Easter. If the wrong equinox date were used, then the wrong day would be chosen for Easter. Other church holidays were also affected by the faulty calendar.

To solve this problem, in 1582 Pope Gregory XIII turned to the scientists of the day, finally accepting a proposal from an Italian physician and astronomer Aloisio Lillo. Following Lillo's advice, ten days were dropped from the calendar. Additionally, to keep the calendar in sync with the actual year, leap years were decreased in number. Previously all century years, in other words, all those ending in 00, had been leap years; now only those divisible by 400 were. Thus, 1600 was a leap year, while 1700 was not. The Gregorian calendar, as it came to be known, did correct the drift of dates and is still in use today.

Clocks and Microscopes

Along with an increasing understanding of the natural world during the Renaissance came inventions. As Bacon observed, "We should note the force, effect, and consequences of inventions, . . . which were unknown to the ancients . . . [such as] printing. . . . For these . . . have changed the appearance of the whole world."[58]

Warfare, for instance, was altered forever with the appearance in the fourteenth century of cannons, and in the fifteenth, of handheld guns. Mathematics provided a description of the paths traveled through the air by cannonballs, enabling cannons to be aimed and directed more accurately.

On a more peaceful note, the period saw the introduction in the mid–fourteenth century of mechanical clocks, run first by weights and then coiled springs. The latter invention led to the first pocket watch, made by the German locksmith Peter Henlein, in 1504.

Along with the telescope, the most important invention of the period was the compound microscope in 1590. Because it had two lenses, this microscope was a more powerful magnifier than a single-lens magnifying glass. Its inventor may have been a Low Countries spectacle-maker, Zacharias Janszoons, although many others claimed credit, including the supposed inventor of the telescope, Hans Lippershey. Beginning in the middle of the seventeenth century, this instrument proved to be the first key to unlocking the secrets of the normally invisible microscopic world.

Modern science was only beginning by the end of the Renaissance, yet its form was already visible in Bacon's writings and in the work of Galileo and others. The rationality and reason promoted by Renaissance researchers would become increasingly important not only to science but all Western thought. Those who came after this period would refine its methods and techniques and open up much more of the natural world to human understanding, but they would always be indebted to the pioneering work of these early scientific thinkers.

The Emerging Modern World

As the Middle Ages had gradually merged with and become one with the Renaissance, so during the course of the seventeenth century did the Renaissance take on the characteristics of the modern age. The modern world would grow out of the political, social, economic, artistic, and scientific trends of Renaissance Europe.

Unlike the pre-Renaissance world, the modern one would be an international arena, in which European civilization and affairs met and often clashed with cultures in the Americas, Asia, and Africa. It would be a world of strong, national states, tied together in tight economic and political nets, and it would be a world built upon scientific principles and technology.

The National Monarchies

Into the 1600s, the political trends of the Renaissance continued. Centralized government retained its strong hold on the national monarchies of Europe, as it would even when the nature of that government changed in future centuries. The German and Italian states, however, remained as fragmented as ever, a situation that would not alter until the nineteenth century.

In England, Elizabeth I died childless in 1603, and the throne passed to the royal family of Scotland, the Stuarts. The Stuart kings, in the best Renaissance tradition, wanted total political control. However, the Stuarts, who were Catholics, soon found themselves in a battle for power

King Charles I, a Catholic whose family ascended the British throne upon the death of Elizabeth I, was executed when civil war broke out in England during the mid–seventeenth century.

Because Queen Elizabeth I (pictured) failed to produce an heir to the throne, the monarchy was passed to the Stuarts of Scotland upon her death in 1603.

with the Protestant-dominated British legislature, Parliament. By the middle of the seventeenth century, this conflict turned into civil war and resulted in a temporary suspension of the monarchy and the execution of King Charles I. Although this monarch-free period lasted only a decade, it set the stage for the eventual reduction of royal power, with political control finally passing into the hands of elected representatives. This democratic process would climax in the eighteenth century with the American Revolution and the creation of the United States.

In France, Louis XIV, who ruled for over seventy years, beginning in 1643, succeeded where the Stuarts had failed. He made the French monarchy supreme. His royal grip on the country and the nobility was so tight that the eighteenth-century French writer Voltaire later said that Louis was the state. This absolute monarchy, however, fell in the late eighteenth century during the French Revolution, whose goals and ideals were similar to those of the American revolt.

Like England and France, seventeenth-century Spain remained a centralized monarchy. However, during this century, the country lost its position as a major European power. An important reason for Spain's decline, from which Spain never recovered, was the nation's dependence upon its New World colonies for income. This revenue, large though it was, was not enough to cover the country's expenses or to create profitable employment for the general population. Spain as a whole had few other sources of income because it lacked any major industry, and the royal government did little to encourage such industry, unlike its counterparts in England and France. Additionally, Spain expelled many of the artisans and crafters who would have formed the nucleus for industry because they were Jews and Muslims, not Catholics.

The East India Companies

The overseas rivalry between European states begun in the Renaissance persisted, as did exploration. However, Portuguese and Spanish domination gave way to English, French, and Dutch supremacy. Portugal and Spain did not disappear from the international scene, but they did lose ground to their northern rivals. The latter took possession of trade routes, colonized large sections of North America, and discovered new lands, such as Australia and Tahiti.

In England, the glow of victory over the Spanish Armada produced an air of optimism. The country's merchants were now determined to establish their own trade with India, and in 1600 the English East India Company was formed to achieve that goal. Although initially small, the company would grow, eventually wresting control of Indian trade from Portugal and coming to rule much of India.

Across the North Sea, the Dutch were also busy with plans for foreign trade. In 1602, following the lead of England, they formed the Dutch East India Company, which was larger than its English counterpart. Like the old Hanseatic League, the company had its own diplomats and warships. The goal of the Dutch East India Company was to gain complete control of the spice trade out of Indonesia. This aim was achieved when the Dutch attacked and drove the Portuguese out of the islands.

England and France in the New World

Even as the English and Dutch East India Companies were making their first voyages to Asia, other overseas ventures were underway. For England, the most important of these was the settling in 1607 of Jamestown, Virginia, the first successful English colony on the American mainland. The Plymouth Colony followed in 1620, as well as others, until England had thirteen colonial regions along the Atlantic coast of North America. From these colonies would eventually arise the United States.

At the same time England was colonizing Virginia, France began settling Canada, establishing the colony of Quebec in 1608; other French-Canadian colonies followed. Quebec and its sister settlements were im-

The pilgrims landed in Plymouth, Massachusetts, in 1620 and established the second British colony in North America.

portant centers in the lucrative North American fur trade. In the eighteenth century, England gained Canada from the French as a spoil of war, although to this day, Quebec and its neighbors see themselves as French rather than English.

New Science

Even as the Age of Exploration proceeded, so did the Scientific Revolution. Seventeenth-century scientists, taking up where Renaissance researchers left off, made many important discoveries. For example, following in the footsteps of Vesalius, the English physician William Harvey published the first accurate description of blood circulation in 1628. Later, in 1676, new and improved microscope lenses allowed the Dutch researcher Antoni van Leeuwenhoek to see living things normally invisible to the naked eye. And, building on the work of Galileo and Kepler, the English scientist Sir Isaac Newton in 1687 formulated the three laws of motion and the law of universal gravitation in his *Philosophiae Naturalis Principia Mathematica (Mathematical Principles of Natural Philosophy)*. The work of these scientists and that of many others transformed natural philosophy into modern science.

The Renaissance is certainly important for having laid the foundation of the present-day world, and yet, even though it

Seventeenth-century scientists were responsible for the Scientific Revolution during which many important discoveries were made. Sir Isaac Newton (pictured), for example, formulated the three laws of motion and the law of universal gravitation.

is centuries in the past, this age is more than an interesting antique. In many ways, it still lives in the rich and lasting legacy of art and literature that it passed down to the current age. As Bergin and Speake write:

> For historians the age of the Renaissance had an ending, as all human things must, but in a deeper and truer sense the Renaissance is still alive. The creations of its great artists are still contemplated with awe, its . . . [writers] are still read and indeed are still "best sellers." [59]

Notes

Introduction: The New Age

1. Charles G. Nauert, *The Age of the Renaissance and Reformation.* Washington, DC: University Press of America, 1977, p. 1.

2. Quoted in Peter Burke, *The Renaissance.* London: Longmans, 1964, p. 6.

3. Quoted in Burke, *The Renaissance,* pp. 21–22.

4. Robert Ergang, *The Renaissance.* Princeton, NJ: D. Van Nostrand, 1967, p. 1.

Chapter 1: Humanists and Culture

5. Ernst Breisach, *Renaissance Europe: 1300–1517.* New York: Macmillan, 1973, p. 314.

6. Will Durant, *The Story of Civilization,* vol. 4, *The Age of Faith.* New York: Simon and Schuster, 1950, p. 443.

7. Crane Brinton, John B. Christopher, and Robert Lee Wolff, *A History of Civilization,* vol. 1, *Prehistory to 1715,* 2nd ed. Englewood Cliffs, NJ: Prentice-Hall, 1960, p. 444.

8. Quoted in Brinton, Christopher, and Wolff, *A History of Civilization,* pp. 422–23.

9. Marsilio Ficino, *The Philebus Commentary,* trans. Michael J. B. Allen. Berkeley: University of California Press, 1975, p. 78.

10. Quoted in Samuel Dresden, *Humanism in the Renaissance,* trans. Margaret King. New York: McGraw-Hill, 1968, p. 11.

11. Nauert, *The Age of the Renaissance,* p. 102.

12. Nauert, *The Age of the Renaissance,* p. 119.

13. Quoted in Burke, *The Renaissance,* p. 28.

14. John Hale, *The Civilization of Europe in the Renaissance.* New York: Atheneum, 1993, p. 191.

Chapter 2: Merchants and Commerce

15. Breisach, *Renaissance Europe,* pp. 319–20.

16. Quoted in Hale, *The Civilization of Europe in the Renaissance,* p. 379.

17. Durant, *The Age of Faith,* pp. 619–20.

18. Ergang, *The Renaissance,* p. 80.

19. Emil Lucki, *History of the Renaissance: 1350–1550,* vol. 1, *Economy and Society.* Salt Lake City: University of Utah Press, 1963, pp. 46–47.

20. Lucki, *Economy and Society,* pp. 52–53.

21. Will Durant, *The Story of Civilization,* vol. 5, *The Renaissance.* New York: Simon and Schuster, 1953, pp. 70–71.

22. Quoted in Lucki, *Economy and Society,* p. 86.

23. Quoted in Brinton, Christopher, and Wolff, *A History of Civilization,* p. 433.

Chapter 3: Rulers and Explorers

24. Brinton, Christopher, and Wolff, *A History of Civilization,* p. 517.

25. Quoted in Donald R. Kelley, *Renaissance Humanism.* Boston: Twayne, 1991, p. 21.

26. Nauert, *The Age of the Renaissance,* p. 97.

27. Niccolò Machiavelli, *The Prince,* trans. Luigi Ricci and rev. E. R. P. Vincent, in *The Prince and the Discourses.* New York: Modern Library, 1950, p. 65.

28. Breisach, *Renaissance Europe,* pp. 175–76.

29. Breisach, *Renaissance Europe,* p. 138.

30. Quoted in Brinton, Christopher, and Wolff, *A History of Civilization,* p. 577.

31. Quoted in Robert J. Clements and Lorna Levant, eds. and trans., *Renaissance Letters: Revelations of a World Reborn.* New York: New York University Press, 1976, p. 367.

Chapter 4: Painting and Sculpture

32. Breisach, *Renaissance Europe,* pp. 357–58.

33. Leon Battista Alberti, *On Painting,* trans. Cecil Grayson. London: Penguin, 1972, p. 72.

34. Quoted in Burke, *The Renaissance,* p. 45.

35. Leonardo da Vinci, *The Notebooks of Leonardo da Vinci: A New Selection,* ed. Pamela Taylor, trans. Jean Paul Richter. New York: New American Library, 1960, pp. 32–33.

36. Ergang, *The Renaissance,* p. 390.

37. Quoted in Emil Lucki, *History of the Renaissance: 1350–1550,* vol. 4, *Literature and Art.* Salt Lake City: University of Utah Press, 1965, p. 215.

38. Alberti, *On Painting,* p. 76.

39. Quoted in Lucki, *Literature and Art,* p. 169.

40. Ergang, *The Renaissance,* p. 386.

Chapter 5: Poems, Novels, and Plays

41. Thomas G. Bergin and Jennifer Speake, eds., *Encyclopedia of the Renaissance.* London: B. T. Batsford, 1987, p. 55.

42. Quoted in Burke, *The Renaissance,* pp. 131–32.

43. Ergang, *The Renaissance,* p. 107.

44. Lorenzo de' Medici, *Lorenzo de' Medici: Selected Poems and Prose,* ed. and trans. Jon Thiem. University Park: Pennsylvania State University Press, 1991, p. 113.

45. Breisach, *Renaissance Europe,* pp. 344–45.

46. Quoted in Bergin and Speake, *Encyclopedia of the Renaissance,* p. 94.

47. Quoted in William Shakespeare, *The Complete Works of Shakespeare,* ed. Hardin Craig. Glenview, IL: Scott, Foresman, 1961, p. 48.

48. Brinton, Christopher, and Wolff, *A History of Civilization,* p. 556.

49. Nauert, *The Age of the Renaissance,* p. 262.

Chapter 6: Science and Medicine

50. Francis Bacon, *Novum Organum.* Chicago: Encyclopaedia Britannica, 1952, pp. 114, 123.

51. Nicolaus Copernicus, *On the Revolutions of the Heavenly Spheres,* trans. Charles Glenn Wallis. Chicago: Encyclopaedia Britannica, 1939, p. 508.

52. Stephen Toulmin and June Goodfield, *The Fabric of the Heavens: The Development of Astronomy and Dynamics.* New York: Harper, 1961, p. 70.

53. Anthony Grafton, "The New Science and the Tradition of Humanism," in *The Cambridge Companion to Renaissance Humanism,* ed. Jill Kraye. Cambridge, England: Cambridge University Press, 1996, p. 205.

54. Nauert, *The Age of the Renaissance,* p. 264.

55. Copernicus, *On the Revolutions of the Heavenly Spheres,* p. 506.

56. Quoted in Clements and Levant, *Renaissance Letters,* pp. 177–78.

57. Quoted in Bergin and Speake, *Encyclopedia of the Renaissance,* p. 27.

58. Bacon, *Novum Organum,* p. 135.

Epilogue: The Emerging Modern World

59. Bergin and Speake, *Encyclopedia of the Renaissance,* p. ix.

For Further Reading

Giovanni Caselli, *A Florentine Merchant.* New York: P. Bedrick, 1986. A fictionalized account of the day-to-day activities of a real life fourteenth-century merchant, Messer Francesco. The narrative gives details about such subjects as business practices and problems, trade networks, art patronage, and marriage customs. The text is supported by the author's well-drawn illustrations and a glossary.

———, *The Renaissance and the New World.* New York: P. Bedrick, 1986. Details the daily lives of people living in several Renaissance states, including Spain, France, England, and their colonies in the Americas. The author's illustrations provide a museum-like tour of everyday tools, glassware, and dress. Included are useful maps, cutaways showing the interiors of ships and of the homes of both rich and poor, and a book list for further reading.

Sarah Flowers, *The Reformation.* San Diego: Lucent, 1996. A well-illustrated introduction to the successor of the Renaissance, its origins and growth. Text is supplemented with excerpts from contemporary writings, a time line, a reading list, and maps.

Nathaniel Harris, *Renaissance Art.* New York: Thompson Learning, 1994. Filled with photographs and reproductions of Renaissance Italian art, this work covers such topics as techniques, perspective, portrait and landscape painting, sculpture, architecture, and religious and classical influences.

Harry Henderson and Lisa Yount, *The Scientific Revolution.* San Diego: Lucent, 1996. A good introduction to the people and ideas that gave birth to modern science. Included also are many illustrations, a time line, excerpts from scientific writings of the period, and a reading list.

Deborah Hitzeroth and Sharon Heerboth, *Galileo Galilei.* San Diego: Lucent, 1992. Traces the life and achievements of Galileo through his own writings and the writings of others. Filled with illustrations, this account is enhanced by a time line and a reading list.

Sarah Howarth, *Renaissance People.* Brookfield, CT: Millbrook, 1992. A good source for learning about various Renaissance occupations, such as princes, artisans, explorers, bankers, and beggars. Plenty of information, some of it from firsthand accounts, is enhanced by photographs and drawings, a glossary, and further readings.

———, *Renaissance Places.* Brookfield, CT: Millbrook, 1992. A useful, detailed look at such parts of Renaissance life as a city, a palace, a library, and a sculptor's workshop. Accompanying the text are drawings and photographs, a glossary, and a bibliography.

William W. Lace, *Elizabethan England.* San Diego: Lucent, 1995. Filled with instructive illustrations, this history of the English Renaissance focuses on the reign of Elizabeth I. It also contains excerpts from period documents, a time line, and a reading list.

————, *Michelangelo*. San Diego: Lucent, 1993. Using Michelangelo's own words, as well as those of other contemporaries, this biography paints a full picture of the life of this important Renaissance artist. Illustrations, including photographs and reproductions of Michelangelo's work, a time line, and a reading list round out the presentation.

Stephen R. Lilley, *Hernando Cortés*. San Diego: Lucent, 1996. Depending upon firsthand accounts, as well as the writings of historians, this biography describes Cortés and his conquest. It also places the man and his deeds in the context of his times and highlights their importance to the development of Mexico. Additional material includes a time line of Cortés's life, a reading list, and numerous illustrations.

Karen Osman, *The Italian Renaissance*. San Diego: Lucent, 1996. Looks in detail at the development of the Renaissance in Italy. Black-and-white illustrations, excerpts from eyewitness accounts, a time line, and additional reading are important supplements to the text.

Daniel C. Scavone, *Christopher Columbus*. San Diego: Lucent, 1992. Using excerpts from Columbus's logs and other writings, this biography digs into the character of the man, his motives, and his accomplishments. The account is supplemented by illustrations, a time line, and a reading list.

Jeffrey L. Singman and Will McClean, *Daily Life in Elizabethan England*. Westport, CT: Greenwood Press, 1996. Explores a typical day in late sixteenth-century England, covering such topics as social classes, house building, clothing, recipes, and songs and games. Supporting material includes illustrations, a reading and video list, and a glossary.

Works Consulted

Leon Battista Alberti, *On Painting.* Trans. Cecil Grayson. London: Penguin, 1972. An important Renaissance technical book on painting, dealing mathematically with perspective and discussing the then-known facts about color.

Francis Bacon, *Novum Organum.* Chicago: Encyclopaedia Britannica, 1952. An important work in the development of the philosophy of science during the Renaissance.

Thomas G. Bergin and Jennifer Speake, eds., *Encyclopedia of the Renaissance.* London: B. T. Batsford, 1987. Hundreds of entries provide good, detailed coverage of Renaissance people, terms, and events. Ends with a useful bibliography, divided by subject, and a time line of major political and religious happenings of the period.

Ernst Breisach, *Renaissance Europe: 1300–1517.* New York: Macmillan, 1973. A thorough survey of all aspects of Renaissance life and culture, supplemented with drawings and illustrations and a massive bibliography ordered by topic.

Crane Brinton, John B. Christopher, and Robert Lee Wolff, *A History of Civilization.* Vol. 1, *Prehistory to 1715,* 2nd ed. Englewood Cliffs, NJ: Prentice-Hall, 1960. The chapters on the Renaissance present a good, clear outline, as well as a balanced account of the philosophical, social, political, and artistic concerns of the period.

Leonardo Bruni, *The Humanism of Leonardo Bruni: Selected Texts.* Trans. Gordon Griffiths, James Hankins, and David Thompson. Binghamton, NY: Renaissance Society of America, 1987. A general collection of the writings of an early humanist, providing examples that reveal Bruni's varied interests and accomplishments.

Peter Burke, *The Renaissance.* London: Longmans, 1964. A useful selection of original writings from the Renaissance, as well as excerpts from later historians.

Benvenuto Cellini, *The Autobiography of Benvenuto Cellini.* Trans. John Addington Symonds. Garden City, NY: Doubleday, 1946. A detailed, fascinating, if not always believable, firsthand account of the life of the artist in Renaissance Europe.

Robert J. Clements and Lorna Levant, eds. and trans., *Renaissance Letters: Revelations of a World Reborn.* New York: New York University Press, 1976. Arranged by subject, this collection of letters from the Renaissance presents firsthand accounts of how the people of the period felt about a variety of matters, such as humanism, education, politics, and art.

Nicolaus Copernicus, *On the Revolutions of the Heavenly Spheres.* Trans. Charles Glenn Wallis. Chicago: Encyclopaedia Britannica, 1939. One of the most important scientific books of the Renaissance, in which the theory of a moving earth and a stationary sun is supported with recorded observations and mathematical analysis.

Dante Alighieri, *The Divine Comedy.* Trans. H. R. Huse. New York: Holt, Rinehart and Winston, 1954. A prose translation that effectively captures the spirit and drama of Dante's poem. The text is supplemented with the translator's notes, a schematic of hell, purgatory, and heaven, and a glossary.

Samuel Dresden, *Humanism in the Renaissance*. Trans. Margaret King. New York: McGraw-Hill, 1968. Filled with reproductions of Renaissance art, this description of humanism is readable and informative.

Will Durant, *The Story of Civilization*. New York: Simon and Schuster.

Vol. 4, *The Age of Faith* (1950);

Vol. 5, *The Renaissance* (1953);

Vol. 6, *The Reformation* (1957). A classic multivolume study written in a readable and accessible style. Filled with facts, incidents, and speculation, and supplemented with a large bibliography.

Desiderius Erasmus, *The Praise of Folly*. Trans. Hoyt Hopewell Hudson. New York: Modern Library, 1941. The Dutch humanist's most popular work, which satirizes many aspects of Renaissance society.

Robert Ergang, *The Renaissance*. Princeton, NJ: D. Van Nostrand, 1967. Traces the development of the Renaissance in Italy, France, Spain, and England. The opening chapters examine the transformation of the late Middle Ages into the Renaissance.

Marsilio Ficino, *The Philebus Commentary*. Trans. Michael J. B. Allen. Berkeley: University of California Press, 1975. This study of Plato by an important Italian humanist provides good insight into how the Renaissance interpreted the ancient Greek's philosophy.

John Hale, *The Civilization of Europe in the Renaissance*. New York: Atheneum, 1993. Written by an eminent historian of the Renaissance, a thorough survey of the thought and art of the time. Photographs and reproductions of Renaissance art and an extensive bibliography support the text.

Donald R. Kelley, *Renaissance Humanism*. Boston: Twayne, 1991. A good examination of the origins and nature of humanism. Ends with a bibliographical essay and a time line of intellectual achievements of the period.

Jill Kraye, ed., *The Cambridge Companion to Renaissance Humanism*. Cambridge, England: Cambridge University Press, 1996. A collection of essays by noted scholars on every aspect of humanism, examining such topics as humanism's relation to art, literature, and politics.

Leonardo da Vinci, *The Notebooks of Leonardo da Vinci: A New Selection*. Ed. Pamela Taylor, trans. Jean Paul Richter. New York: New American Library, 1960. A good selection from Leonardo's notebooks, showing his far-ranging intellect and his vast grasp of Renaissance learning.

Emil Lucki, *History of the Renaissance: 1350–1550*. Vol. 1, *Economy and Society*. Salt Lake City: University of Utah Press, 1963. Provides excellent coverage of all parts of Renaissance commerce, from trading to banking, to manufacturing to farming. The text is supported by a bibliography divided by subject.

———, *History of the Renaissance: 1350–1550*. Vol. 4, *Literature and Art*. Salt Lake City: University of Utah Press, 1965. A good survey of Renaissance art and literature, giving detailed information on painting, sculpture, architecture, drama, fiction, poetry, and the vernacular. Ends with a bibliography divided by topic.

————, *History of the Renaissance: 1350–1550*. Vol. 5, *Politics and Political Theory*. Salt Lake City: University of Utah Press, 1964. Traces political development during the Renaissance, examining the important political theories of the day. The text is supplemented by a topic-specific bibliography.

Niccolò Machiavelli, *The Prince*. Trans. Luigi Ricci, rev. E. R. P. Vincent. In *The Prince and the Discourses*. New York: Modern Library, 1950. One of the most important political documents of the Renaissance, it analyzes the required character of a successful ruler of the period and the problems faced by such a leader.

Lorenzo de' Medici, *Lorenzo de' Medici: Selected Poems and Prose*. Ed. and trans. Jon Thiem. University Park: Pennsylvania State University Press, 1991. A collection of writings by an important Renaissance ruler, showing the variety of his humanistic interests.

Charles G. Nauert, *The Age of the Renaissance and Reformation*. Washington, DC: University Press of America, 1977. Traces the development of Renaissance Europe, providing useful information on all aspects of Renaissance life and ending with a topic-by-topic suggested reading list.

Petrarch, *Letters of Old Age*. Trans. Aldo S. Bernardo, Saul Levin, and Reta A. Bernardo. Baltimore: Johns Hopkins University Press, 1992.

————, *Letters on Familiar Matters*. Trans. Aldo S. Bernardo. Baltimore: Johns Hopkins University Press, 1985. In these two collections of letters can be found the Italian humanist Petrarch's thoughts on almost every conceivable subject, from classical literature to humanism to more personal matters.

————, *Selected Sonnets, Odes and Letters*. Ed. Thomas G. Bergin. New York: Appleton-Century-Crofts, 1966. A good introduction to Petrarch's poetry, particularly the sonnet sequence to Laura, in a readable twentieth-century translation.

François Rabelais, *The Portable Rabelais*. Ed. and trans. Samuel Putnam. New York: Viking, 1946. A thoroughly modern translation that reveals the spirit and charm of this French Renaissance novelist.

William Shakespeare, *The Complete Works of Shakespeare*. Ed. Hardin Craig. Glenview, IL: Scott, Foresman, 1961. The collected plays and poetry of the most famous English Renaissance writer.

Stephen Toulmin and June Goodfield, *The Fabric of the Heavens: The Development of Astronomy and Dynamics*. New York: Harper, 1961. Informatively traces the history of astronomy from the ancient world through the end of the seventeenth century, providing excellent details on the work of such Renaissance scientists as Galileo and Kepler.

Index

manufacturing and,
35–36
transformation of Venice
and, 32
see also banking; East
India companies
Copernicus, Nicolaus, 87,
88, 89, 90, 91
Cortés, Hernando, 53
Crusades, 11

Dante Alighieri, 69, 70–71,
72
Decameron (Boccaccio), 73,
75
Dias, Bartolomeu, 49
diplomacy, 48, 49
Divine Comedy (Dante), 71,
72, 73
Donatello, 59–60
Donation of Constantine,
19
Don Quixote (Cervantes), 77,
78
Drake, Sir Francis, 55
Durant, Will, 14, 32, 38
Dürer, Albrecht, 65–66

East India companies, 98
education, 15–16, 21–22, 23
Egypt, 19
*Elegance of the Latin
Language, The* (Valla), 17,
18
Elizabeth I (queen of
England), 42, 49, 55, 79,
96
England, 39, 40, 41, 42, 66
first colonies of, 98–99
poetic representation of,
82
tension with Spain, 55–56

trade and, 34, 35
see also Spanish Armada;
Stuarts; Tudors
Erasmus, Desiderius, 22–25,
30
Ergang, Robert, 12, 33, 62,
67
explorers, 11, 48–52, 54

Ferdinand (king of
Aragon), 45, 46, 49
Fernel, Jean, 12
Ficino, Marsilio, 20–21
Florence. *See under* Italy
France, 21, 24, 39, 46, 84
control of pope and, 11
first army in, 47
humanist college in, 42
modernizing of, 40, 41,
44, 45
monarchy of, 97
Francis I (king of France),
22, 42
Fugger, Jakob, 38, 39, 40, 54

Galen (Greek physician),
86, 92, 93, 94
Galilei, Vicenzo, 68
Galileo, Galilei, 68, 83,
89–92, 95, 99
heresy trial of, 91
Gama, Vasco da, 49, 51
Germany, 24, 33, 65, 67
Bavaria, 38
political organization of,
46, 96
see also Hanseatic League
Giotto di Bondone, 59, 60
Goodfield, June, 83
Grafton, Anthony, 84
Greece, 19
ancient, 10, 86
rediscovery of culture of,
14, 16–17

Greek language, 16, 17, 21,
22, 23
Gregorian calendar, 94–95
Gregory XIII (pope), 95
Guevara, Antonio de, 93
Guicciardini, Francesco, 25
guilds, 15
Gulf of St. Lawrence, 54
Gutenberg, Johannes, 14,
15

Habsburgs, 39, 40
Hale, John, 26
*Handbook of the Christian
Soldier* (Erasmus), 25
Hanseatic League, 33–34,
35–36, 37, 98
Harvey, William, 99
Hawkins, John, 55
Henry VIII (king of
England), 25, 42
Henry the Navigator
(prince of Portugal), 48,
49
Hogan, Edmund, 49
Holbein, Hans, 66–67
Homer, 16, 21
humanism, 13, 16, 23
Christianity and, 24–25
cultural influence of, 26
Latin scholarship and, 17,
19
universities and, 21–22
wealth and, 28–30
see also science

Iliad (Homer), 21
Incas, 52
India, 35, 49, 51, 98
Indonesia, 51, 98
Innocent VIII (pope), 21,
47

Picture Credits

Cover photo: AKG, London

Archive Photos, 16, 23, 24, 32, 38, 44, 71 (left), 73, 75, 77 (left), 81, 85

Alinari/Art Resource, NY, 11, 59, 60, 62, 71 (right), 84

Art Resource, NY, 64 (left), 94 (right)

Foto Marburg/Art Resource, NY, 58

Giraudon/Art Resource, NY, 79

Library of Congress, 14, 19, 20, 26, 42, 45 (bottom), 50, 51 (both), 86, 89, 90 (left), 94 (left), 97, 98, 99

North Wind Picture Archives, 53, 55, 64, 80

Planet Art, 57, 65 (top)

Scala/Art Resource, NY, 90 (right), 92

Stock Montage, Inc., 22, 31, 33, 34, 35, 36, 45 (top), 67, 77 (right)

About the Author

James A. Corrick has been a professional writer and editor for twenty years and is the author of twenty books, as well as two hundred articles and short stories. Other books for Lucent include *The Early Middle Ages, The Late Middle Ages, The Battle of Gettysburg,* and *The Byzantine Empire.* Along with a Ph.D. in English, Corrick's academic background includes a graduate degree in the biological sciences. He has taught English, tutored students, edited magazines for the National Space Society, been a science writer for the Muscular Dystrophy Association, and edited and indexed books on history, economics, and literature for Columbia University Press, MIT Press, and others. He and his wife live in Tucson, Arizona, and when not writing, he reads, swims, walks, frequents bookstores, and holds forth on any number of topics. He is a member of the Arizona Historical Society and the Tucson Book Publishing Association.